#52-99 BK Bud 10/99

P9-CDY-070

made, not born, he provides a realistic program structured to help attract, retain, and motivate dynamic, capable leaders in executive and middle management positions. Following Kotter's advice, companies can build strong managerial teams necessary not only for growth—but also for survival itself.

JOHN P. KOTTER is Professor of Organizational Behavior and Human Resource Management at the Harvard Business School. He has won McKinsey awards for two *Harvard Business Review* articles and has received the 1985 Johnson, Smith, and Knisely Award for new perspectives on executive leadership, and the 1977 Exxon Award for innovative curriculum design for developing the Self-Assessment and Career Development Program at the Harvard Business School. Professor Kotter has achieved national recognition as an expert on leadership in business with his works *The General Managers* and *Power and Influence.*

HD
57.7
.K67
1988

# The Leadership Factor_____

## JOHN P. KOTTER

SOUTHEASTERN COMMUNITY
COLLEGE LIBRARY
WHITEVILLE, NC 28472

**THE FREE PRESS**

New York

THE FREE PRESS
A Division of Simon & Schuster Inc.
1230 Avenue of the Americas
New York, NY 10020

Copyright © 1988 by John P. Kotter, Inc.

All rights reserved, including the right of
reproduction in whole or in part in any form.

THE FREE PRESS and colophon are trademarks
of Simon & Schuster Inc.

Manufactured in the United States of America

printing number
20 19 18 17 16 15 14 13 12

**Library of Congress Cataloging-in-Publication Data**

Kotter, John P.
  The leadership factor.

  Bibliography: p.
  1. Leadership.   2. Industrial management.   I. Title.
HD57.7.K67      1988        658.4'092        87-19805
ISBN 0-02-918331-6

# Contents

# Preface

For nearly twenty years now, I have been studying the managers and executives who populate complex organizations. My focus has been on a broad range of questions: Who are these people (in terms of backgrounds and personal characteristics)? What are the key challenges they face in their work? What do they actually do on the job? Why are some much more effective and/or successful than others? How and why is that changing (if at all) over time?

This stream of work has led me to be increasingly interested in the subject of leadership. My last two books have explored some aspects of the leadership issue. This volume continues that exploration with a focus on three broad objectives: (1) to articulate a useful way of thinking about leadership in complex organizations, and to help explain why that kind of leadership is particularly important today (Part I of the book tries to satisfy this purpose); (2) to demonstrate why most firms do not have the leadership capacity they currently need (or will soon need) to prosper in an increasingly competitive world (Part II focuses on this point); (3) to provide some ideas for managers and educators that can help them deal with this most important problem (Part III is dedicated to this objective).

The argument developed in this book and the data used to support it evolved from a great deal of field work completed in the 1970s[1] and from four additional projects that were initiated specifically for this manuscript. Those four projects, very briefly described, were:

1. *General Background Interviews*. Approximately 150 managers from forty firms were asked to talk about the various subjects in this book. This was not, in any sense, a "random" sample of executives. Some were sought out because of their expertise; others were interviewed on an opportunistic basis.
2. *The Executive Resources Questionnaire*. Based on information from the interviews and literature on related subjects, a ten-page questionnaire (see Appendix) was developed and given to nearly 1,000 top-level executives. Almost everyone completed the questionnaire (the response rate was over 90 percent). In a later follow-up to the survey, about 8 percent of those who filled out the questionnaire were interviewed about their responses (the methodology is described in more detail in Chapter 6).
3. *The Best Practices Study*. Fifteen corporations whose managements have good reputations were examined to see what they actually did to create stronger-than-average senior management teams. One hundred and fifty executives were interviewed as a part of the project (the methodology is described in more detail in Chapter 7).
4. *The Organizational Change Study*. Over a period of three years, I watched five corporations attempt to improve their capacity to attract, develop, and retain leadership talent. A diary was kept in each case, recording what each firm did and what impact those efforts seemed to have.

This book represents the third in a series of works on leadership in business. The first, *The General Managers* (1982), was a detailed, highly systematic study of a group of successful general managers. The second book, *Power and Influence* (1985), argued that many of the complex skills and personal assets that general managers possess are also needed by a growing number of middle-level managers and professionals, because their jobs are increasingly demanding the kind of leadership required in general management jobs. The present book argues that very few firms have sufficient people with those skills and assets. It also attempts to identify what can and should be done about this increasingly serious problem.

As has been the case in virtually all my professional work, this book has been generously supported by the Division of Research at the Harvard Business School. Early drafts of the manuscript were significantly improved through the advice and counsel of Jerry Abarbanel, Gene Andrews, Paul Axtell, By Barnes, Spike Beitzel, Dale Bennett, Harry Bernhard, Marvin Bower, Richard Boyatzis, Nancy Dearman, Anne Donnellon, Russ Eisenstat, Dulany Foster, Jr., Alan Frohman, Jim Heskett, George Hollenbeck, Jay Lorsch, Morgan McCall, Jr., John Murphy, Howard Nitchke, Mal Salter, Len Schlesinger, Robert Steed, Howard Stevenson, and Bart Van Dissell. I am indebted to each of them.

# Introduction

H. Ross Perot is the kind of person who gets some grudging admiration even from his critics (and he has plenty of critics). After all, it is difficult to ignore someone who started with nothing, built a very successful company, amassed a personal fortune of more than a billion dollars, and seems to stand ever ready to take on noble causes regardless of risk or popularity.

Mr. Perot is also a man of strong convictions. Central among them is a belief that effective leadership is an enormously important factor in the world today, and yet a factor that is all too often missing. Commenting on the U.S. economic situation recently, he framed that conviction in the following way: "Our country cries out for leadership at the business level and the political level. Lack of leadership is the biggest problem we have in making this nation competitive."

By saying "the biggest problem," Perot may well be overstating the issue (overstating issues is probably one of his habits that attracts critics). But this book will argue that considerable evidence suggests the man is nevertheless very much on the right track.

More specifically, I shall argue that the age-old topic of leadership has become more salient recently because of important shifts in the business environment; that leadership is no longer just the domain of the CEO or a few top managers, but is increasingly needed in virtually all managerial jobs; that most firms today have not come close to adapting to this new reality; that successful adaptation requires changes in a few dozen managerial practices; and that such change does not come easily, but when it does come, it can serve as a powerful source of competitive advantage.

That argument, along with the supporting data, is presented in ten chapters (divided into three parts). Chapters 1 through 3 set the stage by exploring how business is changing, why leadership is becoming more important, what "effective leadership" means today, and where such leadership comes from. Part II (Chapters 4 through 6) presents the evidence regarding the magnitude of the leadership problem today, and its antecedents. Part III then shifts the focus of discussion to solutions. Chapters 7 and 8 report a new study of a group of fifteen well-known firms that have reputations for excellence in management, and Chapters 9 and 10 discuss what other firms can do to become more like those fifteen corporations.

At its heart, this book is (1) about developing a leadership capacity in the managerial ranks and is (2) based on fairly systematic field research (see the Preface for a discussion of methods). In this sense, the book, if not unique, is certainly very different from the regular fare on leadership in business. One hopes these differences will serve well the book's two broadest purposes: (1) to help managers and executives more effectively to create a leadership capacity in their organizations and (2) to help those same people usefully think about their own careers and professional development.

To appreciate fully why those objectives are important, one needs first to understand why the ageless topic of leadership has recently taken on renewed relevance. That is where we begin, in Chapter 1.

## PART I

# Leadership in Business Today

# CHAPTER 1

# The Changing Business Environment: Why Effective Leadership Is Increasingly Important Today

Leadership* has always been, and probably always will be, an important factor in human affairs. But recently both the need for leadership in managerial jobs and the difficulty of providing effective leadership in those jobs have grown considerably more than most people realize. Two fundamental shifts in the business environment are responsible.

## THE SHIFT IN COMPETITIVE INTENSITY

The more recent and dramatic shift is a significant increase in what might best be called "competitive intensity."[1] In some cases,

* There is no generally accepted definition of leadership (see Bass [1981], Chapter 1). For the purposes of this book, leadership is defined as the process of moving a group (or groups) in some direction through mostly noncoercive means. Effective leadership is defined as leadership that produces movement in the long-term best interests of the group(s). This definition is generally consistent with those used by Burns (1978), Jennings (1960), and other thoughtful writers on the topic. See Chapter 2 of this book for an in-depth exploration of what leadership means within the context of the modern complex organization.

that is because strong foreign firms have invaded other people's domestic markets. The consumer electronics, automobile, and steel industries are obvious examples. Sometimes it is due to deregulation; in the United States we see this in airlines, telecommunications, insurance, trucking, and banking. The emergence of new technologies is having a similar effect. Microprocessing, for example, has allowed a number of firms to enter the once oligopolistic computer industry as strong new competitors. In still other cases, the new intensity is the result of market maturity or overcapacity, which forces established competitors to fight it out in order to avoid stagnation.

Whatever the source, the new competitive intensity has destabilized companies and even whole industries. It has turned a few cozy oligopolistic arenas into battlefields. It is forcing some firms that practically owned their markets to have to compete once again for customers. It is pushing more and more organizations to pay better attention to changing consumer preferences and new technological developments, and then to adapt, innovate, or risk falling prey to a corporate raider. Overall, it is creating a level of turbulence that is sometimes extraordinary, especially when compared to the 1950s and 1960s.

The case of General Motors is instructive. One doubts if the people who ran GM during the 1950s and 1960s thought they were living in an era of stability and benign competition. But compared to recent years, they surely were. In 1955, GM had two or three real competitors and a growing market. Today the firm has nearly a dozen credible competitors, mostly from outside the United States,[2] a market that is often flat, and an industry plagued by overcapacity. Those shifts in its business environment have created a surge in competitive intensity, which in turn is forcing an often reluctant (and often very clumsy-looking) GM to try to change its ways.[3] And in the recent past, the attempts at change have come big and fast:

- To improve its ability to compete, in 1984 GM initiated its first major reorganization since Alfred Sloan set up the basic corporate/divisional structure in the early 1920s (sixty years with one structure!!).
- Also in 1984, the firm acquired EDS, H. Ross Perot's computer company, shifted thousands of GM employees into the

EDS organization, and then started trying to add and redo computer systems throughout the entire corporation (one can only begin to imagine the chaos created by Perot and his troops).

- About the same time, GM set up a joint venture with arch-rival Toyota in which it essentially turned over an ailing plant in Fremont, California, to Toyota management (GM had not needed joint ventures before).

- In 1985, the firm acquired Hughes Aircraft at the unprecedented cost of *more than five billion dollars* (it also didn't use to have to buy technology and diversified growth opportunities).

- During the same period GM established a new subsidiary (Saturn) which it hoped could develop a car of the future and a whole new approach to car-making (the old methods were not working very well any more).

- After years and years of developing and fine-tuning an incredibly complex system of vertical integration, the firm started shutting down some internal component-making units and buying those components from outside suppliers (they found it was sometimes cheaper to buy parts than to make them themselves).

- After decades of increasing the size of the salaried work force, GM began in 1986 the process of eliminating more than 10,000 of those employed in its North American operation (the pressures to reduce costs have grown stronger and stronger).

The GM situation is interesting precisely because it is not that unusual. Hundreds of firms and dozens of industries have been (or are being) forced to go through major restructurings.[4]

Consider airlines. For years, there was great stability in the U.S. industry, created mostly by government regulation. Route structures generally changed slowly and in orderly ways. Prices changed incrementally and across the board. Acquisitions and start-ups were rare. New concepts about the product were even rarer. Then suddenly, in 1978, when the industry was deregulated, the rate of change took off like a rocket.

Since 1979, dozens of airlines have come into existence, have been acquired, or have gone bankrupt.[5] The fare structure of the industry has changed in very fundamental ways, and specific fares seem to continue to change almost daily. Routes have shifted considerably, and in some cases, so have wages. New ideas, like frequent flier programs, have been developed and institutionalized.

The life insurance industry enjoyed an even longer period of stability than airlines and automobiles. For most of the last century, products and marketing methods changed little or slowly. Firms grew with the population and the economy. If there were a time machine that could transport a life insurance salesman from the turn of the century into 1965, it probably would not require much extra training to make him productive once again. But if he were sent into 1985, it would be an entirely different matter.

Today, the life insurance industry is caught up in the financial services hurricane. Thousands of entities, in addition to traditional life insurance companies, now offer some form of life insurance. Thousands more offer products that are alternatives to life insurance. In an effort to adapt to the new competition, insurance firms are adding new products at an unprecedented pace, acquiring related businesses, changing distribution systems, and trying to become less fat and bureaucratic. The latter often requires laying off central office staff, something that some firms have never done since their beginnings more than a century ago.

Bankers are caught up in a similar set of pressures. Suddenly the competition is no longer a familiar entity or two down the block. Suddenly the competition is Sears, Merrill Lynch, Citicorp (even outside of New York), American Express, a number of Japanese banks, and even General Electric. (Yes, G.E. It made more money in financial services in 1985 than every bank in the United States except for three.)[6]

The same basic changes can also be seen in health care. It seems as if everyone associated with this business in the United States prospered in the 1950s, 1960s, and early 1970s as the industry experienced tremendous growth. Fueled by Medicare, Medicaid, and increasingly generous corporate health insurance plans, health care expenditures went from 4.4 percent of GNP in 1955 to 10.7 percent in 1983.[7] But recently that has changed. Growth of funding has slowed, or in some areas stopped, forcing some firms to rethink completely their methods of doing business.

Autos, airlines, insurance, banking, health care—in industry after industry, the basic pattern is similar. After two or more decades of relative calm in which competition was muted, the intensity of competitive activity has heated up. And in some industries, it will probably get a lot hotter than it is even today. Indeed, as this is being written, a number of Korean firms are planning their invasion of U.S. markets. In Europe, the European Commission is pushing to break up the airline cartel and to decontrol the capital market. In Argentina, President Raul Alfonsin is trying to privatize hundreds of firms that the government owns entirely or partly, in order to make them more competitive. In the Philippines, President Aquino is said to be on a similar path.[8]

*All this activity is forcing firms nearly everywhere to reconsider traditional strategies, policies, and routine methods of doing business. As a result, thousands and thousands of managers and executives are being asked to develop new products, new distribution channels, new marketing methods, new manufacturing processes, new financing strategies, and much more. And literally millions of people are being called upon to help implement those new ideas. Figuring out the right thing to do in an environment of uncertainty caused by intense competitive activity, and then getting others, often many others, to accept a new way of doing things demands skills and approaches that most managers simply did not need in the relatively calm 1950s, 1960s, and early 1970s. It demands something more than technical expertise, administrative ability, and traditional (especially bureaucratic) management. Operating in the new environment also requires leadership.*

## THE GROWING NEED FOR LEADERSHIP

A peacetime army can perform its functions adequately with good administration and good management, as long as there is some sound leadership at the very top. During war, an army still needs competent administration and management up and down the managerial hierarchy, but it cannot function without lots of good leadership at virtually all levels. No one has yet found how to administer or manage people into battle.

In a very similar way, thousands of corporations worldwide are discovering that they need more managers who can help them deal with the economic warfare created by increased competitive intensity. As one perceptive officer in a major U.S. corporation recently said:

> It was a whole lot easier to be an executive thirty years ago. Back then, there were lots of opportunities for growth. Today, there is more competition and our markets are much more mature. When I first joined the company in 1952, we actually had monthly "allocation meetings" in our division, meetings in which we decided which customer got our products. Can you believe that?
>
> Today, we need many more and better leaders than back then, broad people with vision and self-confidence. Without these people, there is no way we will continue to prosper. In some of our businesses, without them we won't even survive.

Evidence supporting that assertion can be found nearly everywhere. Look at manufacturing operations. Not long ago, many plant managers were being asked to get a product out the door on a predictable schedule and at a historically reasonable cost. That required some detailed operational planning, a sensible organization clearly defined, and lots of controls (in other words, good management). Today those same executives are sometimes being asked to reduce costs significantly, introduce productivity-saving technologies, experiment with Japanese-like labor relations techniques, set up new satellites in countries with lower labor costs, shorten the time required to get new products into the manufacturing process, and still more. That is, they are regularly being asked to find new ways of doing things, sometimes even approaches that have no precedent. They are also being asked to get others to make the personal sacrifices necessary to implement those new ways, others who no longer have immigrant mentalities or a general inclination to be compliant in front of authority figures. In those circumstances, good management and administration are no longer sufficient. More and more the need is for leadership in manufacturing.

The same change can be seen in staff operations. "Personnel administrators," who twenty years ago were asked to administer the personnel system and help solve minor personnel problems, are now being asked to provide leadership on human resource issues. They are needed to assist corporate executives who are trying to change their firms' cultures to make them more competitive. They are required to find and implement entirely new compensation systems that will encourage managers to think longer term. They are urged to collaborate with manufacturing executives to try to establish a new climate of labor relations.

More and more, the need for leadership doesn't stop at the executive level either. Corporations are finding that even lower-level managerial, professional, and technical employees sometimes need to play a leadership role in their arena. Competition, for example, is demanding that more and more young project engineers coordinate groups of manufacturing, marketing, and sales managers (people outside of their engineering hierarchy) in developing new products. That, in turn, always requires some leadership from those project engineers. Similarly, competitive pressures are pushing older foremen to help create that new climate of industrial relations; one doesn't change adversarial relationships built up over decades simply with administration or management. Those same pressures are requiring that middle-level managers find and implement ways to cut levels and fat from their staffs. Getting people to accept genuine sacrifices is rarely possible without some leadership from those managers. Lloyd Reuss, an executive vice president at GM, sums up the challenge facing more and more corporations today: "We need more leaders at every level of our organization, from entry-level jobs at our factories right on through the car division general managers and the executive committee."[9]

This is almost a radical shift from only a decade ago, much less two or three decades. In the relatively stable and prosperous 1950s and 1960s, lots of leadership was rarely necessary in personnel, manufacturing, or anywhere. Too much leadership, back then, could actually create problems by disrupting efficient routines. Sayings were even invented to signal that what was needed was stability and control, not bold new initiatives (e.g., "If it ain't broke, don't fix it").

Just as leadership in the government and the military becomes more important in war than in peacetime, leadership in business becomes more important when warfare breaks out in the economic sphere. Increased competitive intensity has created just that kind of warfare.

## THE INCREASING DIFFICULTY
## OF PROVIDING EFFECTIVE LEADERSHIP

At the same time that increased competitive intensity has been producing the need for more leadership at almost all levels in many organizations, a second set of less dramatic forces has been steadily increasing the difficulty of providing effective leadership. They are the forces of growth, diversification, globalization, and technological development, which have been making businesses more and more complex.

PepsiCo is not unusual in that regard. In 1955, the Pepsi Cola Company was a $60-million-a-year soft drink firm that sold its product mostly in the United States and employed around 1,900 people. Twenty-five years later, it was a $6-billion-a-year corporation, with more than 100,000 employees, that sold soft drinks, snack foods (Frito-Lay), fast food (Pizza Hut and Taco Bell), transportation services (North American Van Lines and Lee Way Motor Freight), and sporting goods (Wilson), and that derived a significant amount of money from more than a hundred markets outside the United States. Providing effective leadership to the business in 1955 was probably not easy by any reasonable measure. But providing effective leadership in 1980 was definitely more complex by orders of magnitude.

Digital Equipment Corporation didn't even exist in 1955. In 1985, it sold more than $6 billion worth of products and services to thousands of customers in dozens of different industries. It had 45,000 shareholders, 100,000 employees, and operations worldwide. The National Cash Register Company, today known as NCR, was a relatively low-tech maker of cash registers and related equipment in 1955. By 1985, its business was not only bigger, but it also employed the same numerous high technologies as does Digital (and IBM and others). American Express has had an overseas presence for years now; in 1950 it had 186 offices in thirty-one countries. But that has grown to the point where by 1985 it had more than a thousand offices in 130 countries. In many ways, the different services the firm offers have grown even faster (e.g., investment banking, insurance).

A 1950s-to-1980s comparison at most corporations, even at relatively small corporations, would reveal a similar picture.

Dealing with the typical leadership challenges created by competitive intensity—getting costs down, increasing productivity, improving customer service, keeping quality high, getting new products developed faster—is rarely easy. Dealing with those issues always means producing change. Change creates uncertainty, anxiety, winners, and losers. The resistance generated by anxious people or employees facing real losses is seldom easy to overcome, even in simple situations. But simple is not the order of the day any more. And dealing with those challenges in complicated settings can be enormously difficult.

It is one thing to improve customer service in a sales force that employs twenty people, all working out of the same office. It is a totally different challenge if they number 2,000 (or 20,000) and they work in one hundred (or 1,000) offices spread all around the world. It is one thing to improve productivity significantly if one fundamental technology is used in a manufacturing or service operation. It is a different ballgame altogether if one's efforts must be diffused over dozens or hundreds of different technologies. Getting new products developed and to market presents one set of problems if the market is a relatively homogeneous one (e.g., people living in the Midwest United States). A different and far more complicated set of problems present themselves if there are dozens (or hundreds) of markets that are different in some important ways (e.g., Brazil versus Sweden). Getting most anything changed is far easier if the employee population is reasonably homogeneous. Trying to communicate well to people of many nationalities, to young and old, to MBAs and engineers—that's much more difficult.

The leadership challenge at the very top of complex organizations appears sometimes to be almost overwhelming. Establishing and implementing sensible strategies for businesses is rarely easy. But in many situations today, the technological, competitive, market, economic, and political uncertainties make strategic decision-making horrendously complicated. Conflicts of interest inside the firm, between what is good for the American division versus the European group or the traditional bankers versus the new investment banking department, can also make implementing any strategy a most perilous adventure. Yet, unlike 1955, thousands of executives around the world are facing just those kinds of challenges today.

## THE GROWING CONSEQUENCES OF ADEQUATE OR INADEQUATE LEADERSHIP

Both changes in the business environment—the growing competitive intensity and the increasing complexity of firms—are important by themselves. Each is independently having a formidable impact today. The first has been increasing the need for leadership in more and more jobs. The second has been making the leadership challenge in those jobs more and more difficult to handle well. But it is the cumulative effect of the two changes that is so powerful. Put them together, and the consequences of both adequate and inadequate leadership are taking on a whole new dimension today (see Exhibit 1-1).

In environments where competition is limited by regulation or a cozy oligopoly (or whatever), leadership sometimes seems not to make much difference one way or the other.[10] Factors that economists and sociologists call "structural" are often key. But in an intensely competitive environment, where the capacity to identify and implement intelligent change and to motivate superior performance is central to corporate results, the capacity of management to provide leadership takes on new meaning.

There are, of course, people who think (or rather hope) that the world will quickly revert to the simpler and more stable days of twenty years ago. Among other things, they point to growing protectionist sentiment in some countries, to the problems caused by deregulation, and to corporate downsizing efforts as supporting evidence for their beliefs. They ignore all the forces pushing in the other direction.

The rate of technological development, for example, is not going to slow in the immediate future and may even accelerate, producing even more turbulence in some industries. Multinational corporations are not going to disappear or retreat to home ground. Many will probably become increasingly international in scope, forced by slowed growth in their domestic markets (e.g. Japanese firms). And if the Chinese ever get their economic organizations working well, they could make the "Japanese invasion" of the world, in the 1970s, look small by comparison.

Exhibit 1-1
*The Changing Business Scene and Its Consequences for the Leadership Factor*

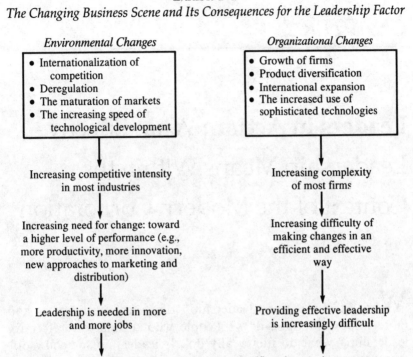

For the rest of this century, we shall probably continue to see a world of business that looks fundamentally different from the 1950s and 1960s. It will be a world of intense competitive activity among very complex organizations. It will be a world in which bureaucratic managers are increasingly irrelevant and dangerous. It will be a world in which even the best "professional" managers are ineffective unless they can also lead. In general, it will be a world in which the leadership factor in management will become increasingly important—for prosperity, and even survival.

It will be a world for which, at least today, most corporations are not prepared.

# CHAPTER 2

# **Leaders in Action:** What Effective Leadership Means Within the Context of the Modern Corporation

W hat exactly is this "leadership" that seems to be more and more important these days? People who demonstrate effective leadership—what do they really do? Is leadership somehow different from "management"? How is it related, if at all, to "entrepreneurship"?

Without some basic answers to those and similar questions, it is not possible to discuss seriously the implications of the changes identified in Chapter 1. Providing such answers is the objective of this chapter.

## DEFINING THE CONCEPT

The word "leadership" is used in two basic ways in everyday conversation: (1) to refer to the process of moving a group (or groups) of people in some direction through (mostly) noncoercive means, and (2) to refer to people who are in roles where leadership (the first definition) is expected. In normal conversation, the second definition is most common. In this book, however, we will usually use the word in the first sense, as a process (not a group of people).

Everyday usage of the phrase "good" or "effective" leadership has even more meanings, but most stress one key point. "Good" leadership moves people in a direction that is genuinely in their real long-term best interests. It does not march people off a cliff. It does not waste their scarce resources. It does not build up the dark side of their human nature. In this sense, one could say Adolf Hitler displayed strong leadership at times, but obviously not effective leadership.

When defined this way, it is usually much easier to identify the presence (or absence) of leadership in any situation than it is to identify whether that leadership is effective. (If you doubt that, ask people whether Truman or Eisenhower provided better leadership while serving as a U.S. president.) For that reason, it is important in any initial discussion of effective leadership in business today to focus on some examples where there is a reasonable degree of consensus regarding the effectiveness dimension. As this is being written in 1987, one such example stands out above the crowd.

## IACOCCA: A STUDY IN LEADERSHIP

Ask people "what single individual has provided the best example recently of effective leadership in business," and by far the most frequent response is: Lee Iacocca. Whether Iacocca really is the best, no one can be sure.[1] Nevertheless, he clearly has provided Chrysler with what many people think is desperately needed in many other businesses.

During the mid-1970s, before Iacocca took over Chrysler, the firm was averaging a return on its assets of about minus 8 percent. In other words, it was in the process of going out of business. In 1984 and 1985, after Iacocca had taken over, created a new senior management team, improved the product, and paid back a huge government loan, ROA for the two years averaged nearly (a positive) 20 percent. No matter what happens to Chrysler in the future, by any reasonable standard that was an extraordinarily dramatic and very impressive turnaround.

Of course, there is some truth to the charges that Iacocca was lucky and that he often gets credit that should go to others. But most observers would agree that good leadership on his part (and on the part of others on his team) was also a very important factor in the turnaround. That is, beneath the surface stylistic indices— the cigar and the gruff voice—one finds a pattern of behavior that is similar in basic ways to Thomas J. Watson, Sr. and a host of interesting historical figures. That pattern, in summary form, is as follows:

1. Iacocca developed an agenda for himself and the firm that included a bold *new vision* of what Chrysler could and should be. It was a vision of a competitive and profitable firm that produced much higher quality products, provided better employment opportunities, and was strong enough to survive in the increasingly competitive automobile industry. It was a vision that valued all the important groups with a stake in the business and tried to meet the legitimate long-term interests of all those groups (customers, employees, stockholders, and others).

The agenda was strategically sound. That is, it contained an *intelligent strategy* for moving the firm toward that vision, a strategy rooted in a broad understanding of what financial, manufacturing, marketing, and personnel matters would have to change. Creating that strategy was no trivial matter. Iacocca was successful here because he was able to draw upon his long experience in the automotive business, his keen mind, and input from hundreds of sources.

2. He attracted, held onto, and elicited *cooperation and teamwork from the large network of people* needed to accomplish that agenda: labor leaders, a whole new management team, dealers, suppliers, some key government officials, and many others. He did so by articulating his agenda in emotionally powerful ways ("Remember, folks, we have a responsibility to save 600,000 jobs"), by using the credibility and relationships he had developed after a long and highly successful career in the automotive business, by communicating the new strategies in an intellectually powerful manner, and in still other ways (e.g., giving people some voice in shaping the agenda). In the process, he created a sense of shared goals and shared fate among people who had often seen their interests as inherently conflicting.

He then worked relentlessly to keep *key people in that network motivated* to work on the evolving agenda, and to work hard. That meant communicating, cajoling, praising, kicking, pushing, pulling, coaching, and inspiring folks, all made possible because of his personal "selling" skills, his high energy level, and a keen insight into the fundamental needs and values that made all those different folks tick.[2]

The combination of an intelligent agenda for change and an energized network of appropriate resources worked miracles. It usually does. We even have research evidence supporting this conclusion.

## BEYOND IACOCCA: RECENT RESEARCH ON EFFECTIVE LEADERSHIP

In 1972, Professor Paul Lawrence and I studied twenty big city mayors. The ones rated the best by both "experts" and voters behaved in much the same way as in the case of Iacocca.[3] In 1978 I studied a group of successful general managers in nine different corporations. Again, much of the behavior of the most effective executives could be summarized by the same two points listed above.[4] Recent work by Bennis, Levinson, and the Center for Creative Leadership paints a very similar picture.[5] Private sector and public, CEO and middle-level general managers, what we find beneath the surface is: (1) a vision of what should be, a vision which takes into account the legitimate interests of all the people involved, (2) a strategy for achieving that vision, a strategy that recognizes all the broadly relevant environmental forces and organizational factors, (3) a cooperative network of resources, a coalition powerful enough to implement that strategy, and (4) a highly motivated group of key people in that network, a group committed to making that vision a reality (see Exhibit 2–1).

In other words, the effective leadership of a project team located ten layers below the CEO in a large corporation and the effective leadership of the overall corporation by the CEO both seem to share some fundamentals in common: a good vision and strategy backed up by sufficient teamwork and motivation. At the CEO level, the vision and strategy will undoubtedly be much more complex, and the number of people from whom cooperation and motivation are needed may be orders of magnitude larger. That is effective leadership with a capital "L." At the project team level, the "vision" may be no more than a slightly new concept for a product, the strategy may be only a series of fairly straightforward steps for developing the concept, the cooperative network might number one boss and a couple of other important people, and the highly motivated core group might include only a few employees.

Exhibit 2–1
*Effective Leadership in Complex Organizations*

I. *Creating an Agenda for Change*

a. Which includes a vision of what can and should be

b. A vision that takes into account the legitimate long-term interests of the parties involved

c. Which includes a strategy for achieving that vision

d. A strategy that takes into account all the relevant organizational and environmental forces

II. *Building a Strong Implementation Network*

a. Which includes supportive relationships with the key sources of power needed to implement the strategy

b. Relationships strong enough to elicit cooperation, compliance, and (where necessary) teamwork

c. Which includes a highly motivated core group of people

d. A core group committed to make the vision a reality

That is effective leadership with a small "l." But it is, nevertheless, still leadership.[6]

It is also clear from this research that despite those key similarities, what it all looks like "on the surface" (exactly how the vision is developed, the motivation created, and so on) can vary enormously. As a group, the mayors, the general managers, Iacocca, and others who have been studied included people who are tall and short, fast and slow, young and old, tough and tender, Democrats and Republicans, brash and reserved, highly participative and fairly directive. Stylistically, there is a great deal of variation; Mary Kay Ash (the chairman of Mary Kay Cosmetics) and Lee Iacocca, for example, look incredibly different, but one could argue that they both have displayed effective business leadership characterized by the points summarized in Exhibit 2–1. No doubt the young project engineer who is buried in Chrysler's bureaucracy and who displays some useful leadership on his project also looks very different from Iacocca. Indeed, if one focuses on style and visible behavior alone in those cases or anywhere, one would have difficulty drawing any general conclusions about effective leadership. It is quite possibly because people often focus on just those points that there is so much confusion today about what constitutes good leadership.[7]

If one does take into account the context, one additional pattern of great importance seems to emerge. Effective leadership, research suggests, is remarkably chameleon-like. What it looks like, on the surface, is very much a function of the situation in which it is found.[8] In a sense, it often seems to "fit" the situation or the key contingencies in the situation.[9] The precise nature of the style–context relationship is not clearly understood, probably because it is very complex. But we have learned something about why it exists, and we shall discuss that more in the next chapter.

Recent research also sheds some light on the debate surrounding the relationship of "management" to "leadership." The research does not put the debate to rest, but it strongly suggests that some of the extreme positions taken in the discussion are not supported by available empirical evidence (e.g., someone who can manage cannot lead, and vice versa). But at the same time, it also suggests that some of the central issues raised in the debate are very important and deserve discussion.[10]

## LEADERSHIP AND MANAGEMENT

Modern management, as it has evolved over the past five decades, can be described in any number of different ways. But at the heart of virtually all such descriptions, one always finds four or five key processes:

1. *Planning*. Planning is the science of logically deducing means to achieve given ends. A variety of techniques have been developed to aid in this process.
2. *Budgeting*. Budgeting is that part of the planning process associated with an organization's finances.
3. *Organizing*. Organizing means creating a formal structure that can accomplish the plans, staffing it with qualified people, defining clearly what each person's role is, providing them with appropriate financial and career incentives, and then delegating appropriate authority to those people. Again, a variety of techniques have been created to aid these processes (e.g., the Hay system of compensation management).

4. *Controlling*. Controlling involves looking constantly for deviations from plan ("problems"), and then using formal authority to "solve" them. This often takes place via "review" meetings. For the financial part of plans, this means using management control systems and the like.

Contrasting this list with Exhibit 2-1 leads quickly to two important conclusions. First, management and leadership are not mutually exclusive. There is no logical reason why a person with the appropriate background and skills could not do both well in some situations. One might even say that the two are complementary and sometimes overlap. Creating agendas that include sound strategies, for example, often requires some planning and budgeting. In a similar way, creating implementation networks that include strong organizations often requires a lot of cooperation from a variety of different sources (e.g., bosses, people in personnel).

But at the same time, management and leadership can be very different. Plans do not have to include a vision (or vice versa). Budgets don't necessarily have strategies (or vice versa). The formal structure an executive has and the network of cooperative relationships he needs can be quite different. Similarly, the process of controlling people and the process of motivating them can be very dissimilar. In a more general sense, management is different from leadership in that it is more formal, scientific, and hence universal. That is, management is more a set of explicit tools and techniques, based on rational reasoning and testing, that are designed to be used in remarkably similar ways across a wide range of business situations.

In this regard, it is useful to look at ITT under Harold Geneen's leadership.[11] As chairman of International Telephone & Telegraph, Geneen used his formal authority in less than subtle ways to get everyone in key jobs to *manage* in a highly disciplined manner. That meant continuously producing detailed plans and budgets aimed at achieving financial objectives set mostly by Geneen (the key objective being 15 percent annual EPS growth). That meant using powerful economic incentives to direct people toward achieving those plans and budgets. That meant establishing elaborate control mechanisms, such as financial control systems and regular business review meetings, and then paying strict attention to the data produced by those mechanisms. That meant doing all of the above in a more systematic and thorough way than was the norm in business at the time.

Geneen got his executives to apply his form of management across a wide range of businesses with great success in the 1960s. During that time, ITT bought dozens of companies and then made them more profitable by managing them more competently. In the process, the firm's revenue went from $811 million in 1960 to $6.36 billion in 1970, while net income grew tenfold ($38 million to $393 million). Overall, that was an incredibly impressive performance.

The problem with this kind of management is that it seems not to work particularly well, except with a lot of leadership, in the kind of volatile and unpredictable environment that competitive intensity has created over the last decade. In that environment, detailed planning, especially financial planning, becomes more and more difficult, if not impossible, to do well (except for the very short term). A managerial emphasis on formal structure, systems, job descriptions, and the like creates a rigidity that often is not capable of responding quickly enough to new competitive thrusts. The tendency to try to control everybody discourages the innovation and the motivation that seem to be so desperately needed in truly competitive environments. All of that eventually can lead to performance problems, which often only increase in size with the application of still more management. And under those circumstances, more and more management can even lead to unethical behavior on the part of people who are under great pressure to meet impossible financial objectives.

That very problem can be seen vividly in ITT's case. With an emphasis on very disciplined management but very limited leadership, ITT has taken a huge fall in the last decade. Its recent financial performance has been among the worst of all large corporations (between 1975 and 1985, ITT income actually went down!).[12]

The phrase "except with a lot of leadership" is key. Strong management tends to be "tight"; with no leadership, it often becomes more and more bureaucratic over time, less and less original in its thinking, and overcontrolling. In a similar way, strong leadership tends to be "volatile"; with no management to control things and to provide reality checks, it can evolve into a certain Jim Jones or Hitlerian madness. Hence, both management and leadership are probably always needed, to some degree, because either in isolation can become perverted.

In relatively stable and prosperous times, limited leadership coupled with strong management seems to work very well (it did for ITT in the 1960s). In times of chaos, strong leadership with some limited management may be what is required. In between, perhaps in times like today, both are probably needed to some significant degree.

## LEADERSHIP AND ENTREPRENEURSHIP

The kind of effective leadership needed in corporations today is also both similar to and different from what is usually thought of as "entrepreneurship." Both, for example, involve risk-taking (in contrast to management, which tends to try to eliminate risk). But unlike effective business leaders, successful entrepreneurs are often very independent, parochial, and competitive. That is fine as long as they are in charge of their own independent businesses (it even helps to some degree). But put them in the middle of a corporation, because of an acquisition, for example, and one finds a predictable set of problems. They seldom enlarge their agendas to take into account the legitimate interests of the rest of their new firm, and they rarely broaden their networks to include other key people in the corporation. Instead, they try to continue operating like an independent business, and sooner or later they end up in a series of more and more difficult conflicts because of this. Put a dozen of those loose cannons inside the same business, and nothing less than a shooting war may ensue.

Indeed, the main reason that some people cannot imagine a corporation in which dozens or hundreds of people play a leadership role is because they equate leaders with that type of entrepreneur. They do not realize, often because they haven't seen any good examples, that there are styles of leadership other than that typically associated with successful entrepreneurs.

My own research on successful general managers strongly suggests that the style of leadership that is effective in most corporations today is one different in some important ways from that supplied by many entrepreneurs.[13] It is a leadership flexible enough and broad enough to take other people's agendas into consideration when developing one's own agenda. It is a leadership that can build support networks not only with subordinates and customers, but also with superiors and peers. It is a leadership that knows not only how to compete (a necessity in an intensely competitive environment), but also how to cooperate (a necessity inside complex organizations). It is a leadership that, perhaps most of all, is *broad* in its vision and in its popular support. It is broad and general in a modern world that tends to create the narrow and the specialized (see Exhibit 2–2).

## *Thinking About Leadership*

Leadership is a murky subject where opinions abound. Nevertheless, it is possible to make some basic statements about what it is within the context of the modern complex organization. The basic conclusions drawn here can be summarized as follows:

1. Effective leadership for some activity in complex organizations is the process of creating a vision of the future that takes into account the legitimate long-term interests of the parties involved in that activity; of developing a rational strategy for moving toward that vision; of enlisting the sup-

Exhibit 2–2
*The Effective Leader and the Stereotypical
Entrepreneur Inside a Complex Organization*

|  | *The Effective Leader* | *The "Stereotypical" Entrepreneur* |
|---|---|---|
| I. Agenda setting | Creates a vision and strategy which takes into account the legitimate interests of other people and groups in the firm. | Creates the vision and strategy which is best for the entrepreneur's group (his "baby"), even if it is not best for the overall firm. |
| II. Network building | Builds an implementation network that includes key bosses, peers, subordinates, and outside. | Builds a very strong and cohesive network of subordinates while sometimes ignoring important peers and bosses. |

port of the key power centers whose cooperation, compliance, or teamwork is necessary to produce that movement; and of motivating highly that core group of people whose actions are central to implementing the strategy.

2. Leadership, in this sense, is generally not the same as what we call "management," although the two are certainly not incompatible (indeed, more and more these days, both are needed in managerial jobs). At its core, management is the process of planning, budgeting, organizing, and controlling some activity through the use of (more or less) scientific techniques and formal authority.

3. This type of leadership is also similar to, yet different from, what many people associate with entrepreneurship. Successful entrepreneurs are often (not always) very independent, strong-willed, and parochial individuals who do not fit into complex organizations well except as the CEO.

4. The type of leadership discussed here is not the exclusive domain of the CEO, or top management. It can be found, and is increasingly needed, at virtually all levels in the hierarchy of organizations. Without it, firms seem to have difficulty dealing with today's competitively intense and complex business environment.

5. What this leadership actually looks like—whether it involves cigars and gruff voices, songs and pink Cadillacs, or something considerably lower-key than either of those—can vary enormously in different industries and at different levels in a corporation. The variations tend to reflect something about the specific context involved (e.g., the type of people, the kind and scale of activity). In a sense, the approach or style associated with effective leadership often seems to "fit" the specific situation in which it is found.

Leadership, in the sense we are using the term here, doesn't match up well with many popular stereotypes or simplistic prescriptions. It is more complex and subtle. Given the incredibly complex nature of today's business environment, that should not be a surprising conclusion.

This final conclusion, along with the ones that preceded it, is important because it informs the next critical step in our analysis: an examination of what personal attributes are needed to produce this kind of behavior. This step is essential, because to appreciate the implications of the contextual changes described in Chapter 1, one needs to know not only what effective leadership means today, but also what is required to supply it.

# CHAPTER 3

# Leaders in Profile: The Personal Requirements Needed to Provide Effective Leadership Today

Everyday discussions of leadership and leaders often have a certain mystical aura. The implication is that people who provide leadership are larger-than-life figures who are beyond rational analysis.

Leadership of the sort needed in corporations today is certainly complex, but it is not beyond our analytical capabilities. It is possible to describe leadership generally; we did so in Chapter 2. It is also possible to talk about its antecedents (e.g., what is required to supply it). That is the objective of this chapter.

## THE NECESSARY PERSONAL ATTRIBUTES

Providing effective leadership, at least in big jobs, is rarely easy. If it were, we would see an abundance of good leadership throughout history. Indeed, even in the simplest conditions a variety of things are needed to create the vision and strategy, and to elicit the teamwork and motivation. But simple conditions are not the norm any more. Complexity is the norm.

It is one thing for an executive to provide leadership on some issue generated by competitive intensity if the group is small and not diverse, the technology simple, the product line limited, and the market homogeneous. It is a whole different matter when large groups of many types of people are involved and when the technologies and products are numerous and complex.[1]

Under conditions of large scale and complexity, the best empirical evidence available[2] suggests that creating an intelligent agenda often demands a knowledge of a truly massive amount of information—about specific products, technologies, markets, and people. Without that knowledge, it simply is not possible to produce good visions or smart strategies, or to judge whether the visions and strategies suggested by others make any sense. It also requires a keen mind, a moderately strong analytical ability, a capacity to think strategically and multidimensionally, and good business judgment to synthesize all that information into a sound agenda. Too often, I fear, we fall into the romantic trap of believing that great vision comes from magic or divine grace. In the business world, it rarely (if ever) does. Great vision emerges when a powerful mind, working long and hard on massive amounts of information, is able to see (or recognize in suggestions from others) interesting patterns and new possibilities.

Under conditions of large scale and complexity, best evidence suggests that attracting and maintaining the large network of resources necessary to accomplish a sound agenda demands enormous credibility, which in turn usually requires (1) a very impressive track record and a good reputation; (2) solid, cooperative working relationships with lots of the relevant players in the industry or company or both; and (3) the interpersonal capacity and integrity that are needed to develop credible relationships with a broad set of people fairly easily and quickly. A handsome face, a quick wit, and a little charisma can certainly help, but those hallmarks of the person who emerges as a leader at a social function are far from sufficient in business. Motivating key people in the network to work hard on the agenda requires a considerable communications capability and a keen insight into all of the different kinds of people involved.

Because of the inherent difficulty of doing all that, effective leadership in senior management jobs also seems to require a tremendous energy level and a deep desire to use that energy for supplying leadership (as opposed to the dozens of other ways that one could use such energy). That implies a highly motivated and self-confident person whose drives push toward the acquisition and use of power to achieve things through others (what psychologists often call power and achievement motivation).[3]

Put all these requirements together (see Exhibit 3-1), and what comes out is a long and complicated list. Given the inherent complexity of the issues with which we are dealing, it is probably not even a complete list. The lesson here is very important, even

Exhibit 3-1
*Some of the Requirements for Effective Leadership
in Senior Management Jobs in Complex Business Settings*

*I. Industry and Organizational Knowledge*

- Broad knowledge of industry (market, competition, products, technologies)
- Broad knowledge of the company (the key players and what makes them tick, the culture, the history, the systems)

*II. Relationships in the Firm and Industry*

- Broad set of solid relationships in the firm and in the industry

*III. Reputation and Track Record*

- Excellent reputation and a strong track record in a broad set of activities

*IV. Abilities and Skills*

- Keen mind (moderately strong analytical ability, good judgment, capacity to think strategically and multidimensionally)
- Strong interpersonal skills (ability to develop good working relationships quickly, empathy, ability to sell, sensitivity to people and human nature)

*V. Personal Values*

- High integrity (broadly values all peoples and groups)

*VI. Motivation*

- High energy level
- Strong drive to lead (power and achievement needs backed by self-confidence)

though it is to a large degree self-evident: Providing effective leadership in senior management jobs in business today requires you to have a lot of things working on your behalf.

Indeed, the reason there seems to be such a small number of people doing what Iacocca helped do for Chrysler is that there are remarkably few people running businesses today who have all the attributes shown in Exhibit 3–1. It is common for executives to be very familiar with certain aspects of their businesses and totally unfamiliar with other aspects, to know some of the key players very well and to be only an acquaintance with others, to have a good but not excellent track record and reputation, and to be very skilled at certain intellectual or interpersonal tasks but not very good at others. Indeed, it is a rare executive today who is truly broad in the sense of Exhibit 3–1. Most are much narrower.

### The Attributes Needed in Lower and Middle Management

The list of characteristics needed to supply effective leadership at lower levels in the hierarchy is, as one would expect, a much less formidable looking document. But it is not really a shorter list.[4]

Even in the smallest of jobs in complex organizations, leadership still requires an understanding of the context, an understanding that is much broader than the technical requirements for the job. It always requires some good working relationships that go behind those dictated by formal hierarchy. It still demands a track record and reputation of some credibility. It always requires some minimum set of intellectual and interpersonal skills. Integrity is relevant for the same reasons it is important in bigger jobs. So is some minimun energy level and desire to lead. In other words, although one does not need Superman-like natural abilities to provide effective leadership in modest managerial or professional jobs today, one still needs a lot of other things working on one's behalf.

Part of the reason it is so hard to find lots of good examples of effective leadership at lower levels in the hierarchy is that so few people possess even this more limited list of assets. Once again, what we often find is a certain narrowness of ability and career experience, a narrowness that undermines efforts to develop visions and strategies and to elicit cooperation and motivation. (Another part of the reason relates back to upper management and its willingness to allow people below them to lead. More on this later.)

## A CONTRAST: THE CHARACTERISTICS NEEDED FOR MANAGING

To appreciate more fully the list shown in Exhibit 3-1, it is useful to consider what a comparable list would be for effective "management" alone within senior management jobs in complex settings.

The knowledge requirements (point I), first of all, are quite different. Effective management demands a considerable knowledge of the disciplines that make up modern management: techniques for planning, organizing, budgeting, controlling, staffing, and the rest. Unlike leadership, it does not necessarily require an extensive knowledge of the situation being managed. The whole concept of the professional manager who can manage anything is based on this point.

The relationship requirements are also different and, in a sense, much simpler. Managerial jobs are assumed (if they are designed correctly) to provide sufficient formal authority over people from whom one needs cooperation. In managerial terminology, that has been traditionally captured in the phrase: Formal authority should be commensurate with responsibility.[5] When that is so, someone should be able to step into a managerial job with no organizational or industrywide working relationships and still perform well the managerial aspects of the job. Once again, this relates to the concept of the professional manager who can move anywhere.

It is not entirely obvious if effective management, like leadership, has any real background requirements (point III in Exhibit 3-1). Managerial experience certainly helps, just as prior experience helps in any job or profession. But one can imagine someone doing an excellent job of planning, organizing, and controlling without having the reputation and relevant track record that provide leaders with essential credibility.

In terms of abilities and skills (point IV), managers clearly need some minimum analytical ability, memory, and judgment. But there is nothing inherent in the management function that requires the same strong interpersonal skills that seem to be so necessary for leadership.

In terms of the final two points, values and motivation, it is difficult to say how different the requirements for management and those for leadership are. A considerable energy level is probably needed for both in complex settings, although the motivation that drives it may be different (for management, perhaps a need to control things?). Integrity, too, is probably important for both, although possibly more so for leadership.[6]

Overall, then, the personal requirements for effective management are both different from and, in many ways, much simpler than those for leadership. This is not to say that it is always easy to provide effective management in complex settings. It most certainly is not. But, relatively speaking, it requires considerably more to provide effective leadership.

But, at the same time, this analysis reinforces an earlier conclusion (from Chapter 2) that there is nothing inherently in conflict between the two sets of requirement. In other words, there is no reason why someone could not have the attributes needed to provide both effective management and leadership in some situation. But the combined list is a very long one. In light of the increasing need for managers who can both manage and lead effectively, this conclusion has some obviously important implications.

## ORIGINS

Pushing that line of analysis one more step, one would ask: Where do all these personal characteristics come from? How many (if any) arrive at birth? Which (if any) are developed early in childhood, in school, or as a part of one's career?

Only a cursory examination of Exhibit 3-1 is needed to provide some tentative answers to those very important questions. Specifically:

- A few of the leadership attributes do seem to arrive at birth: some basic mental and interpersonal capacity (a part of point IV), and perhaps some physical capacity that is related to energy level (a part of point VI). Furthermore, a few of the other attributes build off that native capacity (e.g., some intellectual skills would not develop without some minimum intellectual capacity). Nevertheless, the old homily "Leaders are born, not made" gets little support from this analysis, because most of the items in Exhibit 3–1 come after birth and are not deterministically a function of natural abilities.

• Some of the characteristics are undoubtedly developed relatively early in life. Much in points V and VI (relating to values and motivation) fit this description, as do some items in point IV (abilities and skills). One might say that when it comes to leadership, a knowledge of Freud (who emphasized early life experiences) is a useful, but not a sufficient, condition.

• Few of the attributes seem to be developed by our educational system. Aside from some narrow intellectual skills, none of the items in Exhibit 3–1 is systematically developed to any significant degree in most schools today,[7] including graduate schools of business. This is not to say that schools are incapable of doing more. They simply choose not to do more.

• A surprisingly large number of the items are developed on the job as a part of one's posteducational career. Almost all the knowledge, relationship, and background requirements fit this generalization (points I, II, III). Some of point IV (skills and abilities) and point VI (motivation) does too.[8]

Exhibit 3–2 summarizes these points visually.

The deductions visualized in Exhibit 3–2 are consistent with my own empirical study of effective general managers.[9] To account for why they were able to do what they did, a significant portion of which was providing effective leadership, it was necessary to trace their experiences from birth, through childhood and education, and on into their careers. It was the accumulative effect of those many experiences that gave them the assets needed for leadership.

Once again, it is useful to contrast these conclusions briefly with the most likely origins of the attributes needed to provide effective management. The contrast is helpful because, once again, there are some important differences.

Although the requirements for management have some elements that are innate (basic mental capacity) and some that relate to early childhood (motivation), a major (if not the main) requirement comes from either education or work experience (the knowledge requirement). In the past, a knowledge of the various man-

Exhibit 3-2
*Origins of the Characteristics Required to Provide Effective Leadership*

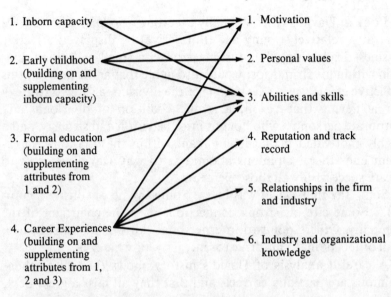

*Origins*

*Personal Requirements Needed
for Providing Effective Leadership*

1. Inborn capacity

2. Early childhood
(building on and
supplementing
inborn capacity)

3. Formal education
(building on and
supplementing
attributes from
1 and 2)

4. Career Experiences
(building on and
supplementing
attributes from 1,
2 and 3)

1. Motivation

2. Personal values

3. Abilities and skills

4. Reputation and track
record

5. Relationships in the firm
and industry

6. Industry and organizational
knowledge

NOTE: Primary effects only (e.g., the weaker causal links [from education to personal values, for example] are not shown in the exhibit).

agement disciplines was learned mostly on the job. More and more these days, it is learned in shorter but more concentrated periods of time at universities or in corporate training sessions. In the last twenty years the amount of such training consumed in the United States has gone up astronomically.[10] Apparently, both corporations and individuals interested in managerial careers have concluded that such training constitutes a better way to learn the fundamentals of management than traditional methods.

## DAVID CONNOLLY: AN EXAMPLE OF A YOUNG BUSINESS LEADER

David Connolly* is typical of the people this writer has met who have displayed effective leadership in a complex business enter-

*A disguised name.

prise. On the surface, it is rarely apparent why people like David are able to do what they do. Those who know them usually offer a diverse range of opinions, but a careful analysis of the situation almost always leads to conclusions consistent with Exhibits 3-1 and 3-2.

Look at David's case. Virtually everyone who knows him agrees that at a relatively young age (thirty-five) he displayed effective business leadership while turning around a small and ailing division within his firm. Most would also agree that at the heart of this effective effort was a new vision for the division, a shrewd strategy for achieving that vision, a strong coalition of divisional and corporate personnel who bought into the vision and strategy, and a highly motivated management team within the division. Agreement ends there. Opinions abound as to why David was able to create successfully all those elements.

Some say that David was lucky. Some say he was just a "natural." Some cite his strong connections with the chairman of the company. Others point to interpersonal skills or his intelligence. Still others point to his drive (or integrity, or whatever).

A careful analysis of David's history shows that all of those opinions are partially correct, and that they all miss a great deal, too.

David was the first of five children born into a middle-class family. His father was a manager in a large organization. From an early age, David was seen to be very bright and energetic. Interpersonally and emotionally, he seemed quite "normal"—neither awkward and troubled nor a "natural leader" and social butterfly. Because of his intellectual capacity, emotional evenness, and energy, he did very well in school. That allowed him to get into an excellent private high school, a prestigious university, and a top MBA program.

David went to work as a financial analyst at AX Industries immediately after receiving his MBA degree. For nearly five years, he worked on various projects in a small staff group that reported to the chief financial officer of the corporation. The work was not particularly exciting, but it played to David's most obvious strength—a keen mind, well trained in economics and business matters. Because he performed well, he was given bigger and broader projects, including some acquisitions studies. Those studies, in turn, allowed him to get to know some of the senior people at AX, plus the firm's lawyers and investment bankers. During that period, some people found David to be arrogant and insensitive to people issues. No one thought of him as a "leader." Those opinions did not interfere with his work, however, because he was essentially in an individual contributor position.

Just before David's fifth anniversary at AX, the new chairman of the board read one of his reports and was so impressed that he invited David to work for him as a personal assistant. David accepted with enthusiasm and stayed in that role for nearly three years.

As an assistant to the chairman, Connolly got an unusually broad overview of the functions and businesses that made up AX. He also got to know the entire senior management and had the opportunity to watch them up close, including those who were the very best leaders in the firm. In this job, Connolly continued to develop his reputation as someone who did very good work. He also began to develop a little humility and sensitivity.

David was next assigned as an assistant to the financial vice president at AX. In that job, he was given a multi-million dollar portfolio to manage, and he continued to do special projects for the chairman. More and more he also began to take part in the process at the very top of the firm; he now not only attended some meetings, he began participating in them.

After two years in that role, the chairman asked David to work as an assistant to the group vice president in charge of AX's rapidly growing businesses. One of those businesses, Zodiac, was a small division (fifty employees) that was losing money. Six months after David started working for the group vice president, the head of Zodiac was fired, and David was installed as the new division manager.

Many people inside AX were surprised that David, a young employee with no line management experience, was placed in the job of a division general manager. Even more people were surprised when he succeeded in that role; by the time he left three years later, Zodiac had a new management team, a sounder operation, better products, and a healthy bottom line. How in the world, some wondered, did that arrogant young man with little relevant experience provide such strong business leadership?

The answer, in general, was that David brought to Zodiac a wide range of assets not possessed by his (fired) predecessor. The previous GM knew parts of the Zodiac business well, but he didn't have the broad perspective on the industry that David had gained in his earlier work analyzing that industry (and others) and in his participation in top management meetings. He also didn't have David's contacts at the highest levels at AX, his strong reputation in the firm as a boy wonder, his keen mind or analytical skills, or (after two years of failures at Zodiac) his energy level. And he had never really had the chance in his entire life to observe a capable business leader up close.

David used the additional assets he possessed to make things happen in ways his predecessor could not. He used his relationships and reputation to get from corporate and divisional people a degree of cooperation that had eluded the previous GM. He used his industry knowledge, his appreciation for top management goals, his keen mind, his analytical abilities, and his many contacts to produce a better vision and a clearer strategy. He used his general leverage inside AX to upgrade the quality of the Zodiac staff, a staff which became very motivated within the context of the new vision, strategy, and level of corporate cooperation. Once events began to move in the right direction, the momentum itself seems to have carried the day.

David also learned some important things in this assignment, especially about the interpersonal skills involved in leadership. Most of his remaining arrogance seemed to wash away. His reputation, track record, and self-confidence grew even larger. All of that added to his capacity to provide additional leadership in still larger positions at AX in the future.

It is never possible to say with much precision why someone like Connolly was able to provide effective leadership in a business situation. But, as in this case, a careful analysis usually leads to the conclusion that the vision, strategy, coalition, and motivation would not have been possible without certain knowledge, relationships, track record, reputation, abilities, motivation, and energy, which in turn were the culminative product of natural abilities, childhood experiences, education, and a number of very important career incidents.

## SOME IMPLICATIONS

It is essential to consider, as we have in this chapter, the characteristics needed to provide effective leadership today along with their origins, because such analysis leads to any number of important implications.

First of all, it confirms the commonsense notion that not everyone has the potential for leadership. Natural abilities and early life experiences eliminate some people, perhaps many. But even if 99 percent of the population on earth didn't have the minimum intellectual capacity, interpersonal skill, motivation, integrity, and energy level needed (which is doubtful), that would still leave millions of candidates who might be able to help corporations deal with the increasingly competitive and complex business environment. In other words, the elitist notion that it is inherently impossible to create large numbers of managers who can provide some leadership gets no support here.

Nevertheless, this analysis suggests that the process of creating strong management teams with leadership capacity is probably much more difficult than the process of creating teams that can just manage competently. Best evidence suggests that the development of an effective business leader is a more complicated matter than the development of an effective business manager (which, by itself, is no simple matter). More complex still is the development of an effective business manager who can lead.

*These implications are important because they collectively suggest that adapting to the new business conditions discussed in Chapter 1 may well be very difficult (although not impossible) for firms.* There is no reason to believe from the analysis presented here that it will be easy to turn a typical group of managers into a human asset that can both manage and lead. There is good reason to believe that turning around a very weak management group should be extremely difficult. If that group lacks certain needed attributes associated with motives, central values, or basic skills (which is often the case), no amount of time and money and effort can change that fact. Those are the product of genetics and early life experiences. One could, of course, recruit an entirely new group of executives who have those assets, but even the very best potential outside hires will usually lack the knowledge and relationship requirements (points I and II). That is, they will not know enough about the company, its culture, and its people to create a sound agenda, nor will they have enough good working relationships with people in the firm to develop an adequate implementation network. And developing those requirements (and others) in a large group of outsiders or younger insiders, the analysis here suggests, might take years and years if the firm is at all complex.

In Part II of this book, we shall empirically test those conclusions. We shall also try to clarify further the exact nature of the leadership challenge facing firms today. Later, in Part III, we shall begin searching explicitly for effective ways of dealing with the challenge.

## PART II

# When Leadership Is Missing

# CHAPTER 4

# The "West Products" Case:
# An Examination of a Firm
# with Insufficient Leadership

It is widely believed that the kind of effective leadership described in Chapters 2 and 3 is sometimes missing altogether in firms. Of the corporations this author has studied closely in the past two decades, West Products[1] is fairly typical in that regard. That is, even though astute observers of the firm cannot produce any precise measures, they nevertheless all seem to agree that in the late 1970s West's management was not capable of providing effective leadership. They further agree that episodes such as the Gerald Stanton story say a lot about why West had such insufficient leadership, and what impact that had on the firm.

## THE GERALD STANTON STORY

West was one of the first modern consumer product companies in the United States. It began with a single product. By 1975, that had grown to four major product lines and a string of retail stores in the Southwest.

In commenting on West Products, an industry analyst had the following to say back in 1978:

West has been a highly successful company in the past, perhaps even too successful for its own good. It dominated some of its markets to such an extent during the earlier part of this century that it never had to be a particularly aggressive or keen competitor. In the last decade this has undoubtedly hurt them.

Although West is still a profitable and important competitor, it is no longer the premier organization in its markets. Today there are other companies that are more aggressive, that are quicker to bring out new products, and that are more profitable. Although the senior management at West has been trying to take corrective actions in the last five or six years, the company is still too centralized and bureaucratic for its own good, and it still has too many long-term employees who are not able to perform well in the newly competitive environment.

The weakest part of West Products is their retail division. Many of us think that the retail group is breaking even or losing money, and we wonder why West hasn't gotten out of the retail business. Of course, the retail division is a very visible part of the firm, and it does allow for an important distribution channel, but its current management seems to be having trouble making it profitable. They also seem to have difficulty attracting and retaining good young people.[2]

In 1978, the most obvious exception to that personnel problem in retailing was Gerald Stanton. Stanton had joined West shortly after graduating with an MBA degree from a university in Texas. After a short initial assignment, he was made a department manager in one of West's retail stores. Well before his thirtieth birthday, he was promoted to store manager, making him the youngest person in that role in the history of the division. Two years later, he was promoted into a staff job within the retail division at division headquarters. One year after that, he was made manager of advertising and sales promotion, reporting to the vice president of stores.

Stanton's initial rise in the organization was unusually quick by West standards; most store managers were in their forties. He seems to have achieved such a fast track by establishing himself as a very bright, hard-working young man. He developed a reputation for spotting and solving problems that others didn't even see. His bosses described him as goal-oriented, good with numbers, honest, and with a good sense of humor. The only "weakness" listed on his performance evaluation was under the heading "delegation," but his management thought he could learn to delegate well over time.

Stanton was much less impressed with his bosses. Many of them struck him as visionless and uninspirational. Furthermore, the huge bureaucracy his superiors embraced was an unending source of annoyance. But he suffered quietly, because his career seemed to be progressing so extremely well.

On January 10, 1978, Stanton was sitting in a routine meeting at West's corporate headquarters in Dallas when his boss, Floyd LaPatta, called him outside. LaPatta said he was being transferred immediately to another division at West Products and was going to recommend that Gerry take over his current job. For Stanton, that meant a sizable increase in responsibilities. He was then supervising a dozen staff people. A promotion into LaPatta's job would mean that he would supervise approximately six hundred people, that his budget responsibility would go up astronomically, and that he would be one of the two youngest vice presidents within West Products. LaPatta told Stanton that if he had any reservations about such a move that he should make them clear within the next twenty-four hours before LaPatta made his recommendation to corporate management.

The position offered to Stanton reported to sixty-two-year-old Joe Clark, the head of the retail division (see Exhibit 4-1). Clark had been with West Products for nearly thirty-five years and had been head of the retail division for ten. Before taking over his present responsibilities, he was within the merchandising part of the business for twenty years after beginning his career at West in one of the stores. Since the early 1970s, Clark had been active outside the company in a number of industry associations. He traveled extensively, and when he was away, the vice president-stores was informally left in charge of the division. Most people at West thought Clark was the weakest and least respected member of top management and had been allowed to remain in his job only because he was close to retirement.

Eighteen people reported to the vice president-stores, most of those being managers of the larger stores. One person reporting to this position, the assistant vice president-stores, served as a second in command.

The job description for the vice president-stores position listed numerous "duties" and concluded by saying that the incumbent was "responsible for the overall well-being of the retail stores." The position was treated by accounting as a cost center (profitability was calculated for the division as a whole).

Exhibit 4-1
*A Partial Organization Chart of West Products*

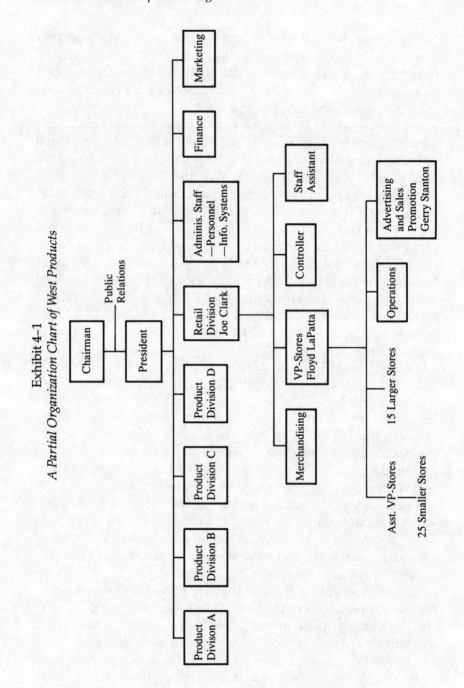

It didn't take Stanton very long, once he began to focus on his situation, to conclude in his own mind that he only had two realistic options: take the job or leave the firm. Not accepting the "offer," he was certain, would put him in what his fellow employees called "the penalty box."[3]

Stanton was formally offered the job Monday morning at 9:30 A.M. He accepted on the spot, and by noon an announcement was made to the rest of the firm. "Commencing immediately," the notice read, Stanton would be vice president of stores in retail, and his former boss would take over a key vice presidency in one of the product divisions (replacing someone who unexpectedly resigned the previous Thursday to take a lucrative job with one of West's competitors).

During the next six weeks, Stanton worked ten to twelve hours a day, trying to get control of this very challenging assignment. He began by analyzing his division's industry and the implicit (there was no explicit) strategy employed by the division to compete. He examined technological and market trends and drew some basic conclusions about why the division was having performance problems. He developed the beginnings of a competitive approach, implicit in which was a fundamentally new vision of what the retail division should be. And then "it" happened.

At seven o'clock one morning, he received at his home a call from the corporate senior vice president in charge of public relations. "Have you seen today's morning paper?" the voice on the other end of the phone barked. No, Stanton had not. "Well get one and be in the president's office for an 8:30 meeting."

The front page of the Dallas paper, Gerry soon learned, was devoted almost entirely to a tantalizing tale about one of West's retail outlets. The police, the story said, raided that outlet late the night before, based on information provided by "a former West employee." Police secured evidence during the raid of "illegal financial manipulations involving" a considerable amount of money.

At the 8:30 A.M. meeting, Stanton found himself in a room with a dozen people, most of whom were relative strangers (the senior management at West had offices on a separate floor, had their own special dining room, and rarely interacted with young managers). It quickly became clear that *he* (his boss was out of town) was expected to "clean up this mess" as fast as possible, minimize the financial damage, get West off the front page, and make sure any employees involved were correctly identified and prosecuted.

For the next four weeks, Stanton got an on-the-job education in crisis management. For twelve to fourteen hours a day he worked with the police, the press, the auditors, corporate PR people, and others in an effort to carry out his mandate. It was tough. Gerry had never faced anything remotely like that before, he did not know most of the people from whom he now needed help, and he received virtually no assistance from his boss (who seemed to go out of his way to put distance between himself and the crisis). All thinking about a new vision of the retail division was shoved into a desk drawer and completely ignored. There was no time for that.

Through a combination of determination, hard work, intelligence, and luck, Stanton emerged from the incident tired but successful. Some of the firm's top management were very impressed by his capacity to deal with a difficult situation. He, too, developed some additional self-confidence in the process.

With the crisis behind him, Stanton once again began work on retail strategy. His lack of experience in any of the product divisions proved to be a problem when he was trying to develop new product concepts for the stores, but he pushed ahead anyway, relying on his keen mind and a great deal of hard work.

Slowly, over a six-week period, some basic ideas became clearer and clearer to Stanton. To test their feasibility, he began appraising whether his organization was capable of implementing those ideas. That part of the analysis was relatively easy. His organization, he concluded, was not up to the task.

Almost all of the management in the stores organization joined West after graduating from local high schools and community colleges. Many were hired into relatively low-skill jobs in the stores and were promoted to assistant department manager, department manager, and then store manager (all in the same store). The few people hired who were like Stanton usually became frustrated and left West before reaching the store manager level.

Stanton drew up an organization chart, one that reflected his new concept of how the division might be run. Predictably, the chart had many boxes with no names in them. Just as he was about to go to Corporate Personnel to talk about the situation, crisis number two emerged.

It seems that one of the product divisions had just spent a considerable amount of money increasing manufacturing capacity for what appeared to be a very popular new product. Then someone discovered that the product was selling ten times as fast through West's retail outlets than through other means of distribution—an unprecedented situation. And then someone discovered why. It wasn't selling very well at all, it was stacking up in the back of an out-of-date warehouse, undetected by an unusually weak inventory control system.

The teeth-gnashing, name-calling, and long, difficult meetings went on for nearly two months. Once again, Stanton's attention was drawn away from longer-term issues to a difficult and costly problem. He tried to obtain assistance from others in his group so that the crisis did not absorb all his time, but he still wasn't very skilled at delegating, and there were few capable people who could really help. The single most capable person, the assistant VP-stores, didn't cooperate with much enthusiasm. His attitude seemed to be, "Well, they gave you the VP-stores job instead of me, so *you* do it!"

Stanton came out of this crisis with some real battle scars. By the time the incident was resolved, he was physically exhausted. His credibility with top management and his own people had dropped, and he had made a few important enemies in that one product division. All of this fortified his resolve to change the people and practices that were creating those crises.

On June 21, Stanton sat down with Joe Clark, his boss, and spelled out his analysis of the division's problems, along with what had to be changed to solve those problems. It was the most difficult meeting he had ever attended. Thirty minutes into the discussion it was clear that his boss, sensing the sweeping implications, was not pleased to hear his analysis. After an hour, Mr. Clark began to debate Gerry on trivial side issues, derailing his carefully thought-through presentation. At one point, when Clark was particularly flustered, he blurted out: "Why have you been working on a new strategy for the stores? That's not your job." After two hours, and before Stanton could finish his entire presentation, Clark stopped the meeting with an excuse about another forgotten appointment. The meeting, Stanton correctly concluded, was a disaster.

A week later, he made some specific personnel requests: one demotion, one firing, and two promotions for young (but bright and eager) employees. His boss said he wanted to study the ideas for a while, and talked about a few dozen "personnel policies" that might make it difficult for Gerry to act. Then he left town for three weeks.

Stanton sought help from Corporate Personnel. One person on that staff tried hard to be of assistance in finding capable people in other West divisions. But nothing happened. There were always excuses about why it was not a good idea to move someone into the retail division, even high-potential people with very narrow backgrounds that clearly needed a broadening experience.

Then another crisis developed. The details are not important for our purposes here. Once again, it absorbed most of Stanton's time and energy. When it was over, he tried once again to get his boss to consider some major changes. But he failed. And then another crisis developed.

Two years after Stanton took the store vice president job, his boss retired. A senior executive in charge of one of the product divisions was brought in to head retail. That person spent three months assessing the situation and concluded that Stanton had done only a marginally acceptable job for the last two years. "The stores need a new strategic direction, and the store organization needs strengthening," the new boss said, "and you have made precious little progress on either of these top priorities." That kind of performance was not good enough, he told Stanton, and he moved him into a less important position. He then brought Floyd LaPatta back to be, once again, the VP-stores.

Stanton tried to get a hearing for what he thought was a very unfair decision, but he ran into an unresponsive and timid personnel bureaucracy.

He remained in his demoted position for only a short time and then left the company. At a personnel planning meeting four months later, someone asked why such a promising young employee ended up leaving. No one at the meeting seemed to want to discuss that question for long.

## THE UNDERLYING PROBLEM AT WEST

This single story in the history of West Products has been described at some length for three reasons: (1) In the late 1970s, events at West all too frequently had many of the same characteristics of this tale; (2) it is closely related to West's leadership problem; and (3) this type of story can be found at many firms that have very weak leadership.

The story was a common one at West not because most managers looked like Stanton; far too many looked more like Joe Clark. It was common in the following ways:

- The managers inside West with leadership potential often left the firm because of frustration, neglect, or abuse.

- Managers at almost all levels who tried to provide the firm with needed leadership often ran into an unresponsive bureaucracy or barriers constructed by their own bosses.

- Jobs in lower- and middle-level management often had a large "firefighting" component to them, which prematurely aged people and did little to prepare them for the strategic and organization-building tasks associated with more senior-level jobs.

- Because the firm had virtually no depth of management, it often pushed managers into higher-level jobs for which they were not prepared.

- Most managers found it almost impossible to move people across division lines (the LaPatta story was an exception) as a way of developing people or building organizations.

- When managers tried to strengthen the team that reported to them, they often found barriers caused by a weak entry-level recruiting effort.

- Managers rarely got the coaching and support from their bosses that they needed to develop themselves or their organizations.

- A manager who did not accept a "promotion," even if it made little long-term sense for the individual or the firm, rarely received another offer for promotion for years (if ever).

Those practices, and many others like them, were the norm at West. No one in the firm defended them, although many senior managers downplayed how prevalent they really were. One senior executive even criticized that way of operating in a number of speeches, and a few personnel managers tried to develop "programs" for producing more sensible results. But that way of operating persisted, despite the good intentions of that one senior executive and the personnel programs, because it was created both directly and indirectly by two forces of enormous power:

1. Short-term business pressures (e.g., someone in a key job quits, the job is essential to meeting quarterly targets, but no one has been developed to be that person's backup, so the best available candidate is grabbed from somewhere else in the organization, and because he or she has no ready backup, someone is shoved into a job for which he or she is not prepared).
2. Parochial politics (e.g., someone has job openings that would be excellent development opportunities for people in other divisions, yet cannot fill any of those slots because bosses in other divisions don't want to give their good people away, or are unwilling to fill the slots with outsiders either because the jobs have been promised to insiders or because of a fear that the outsiders will be someone else's rejects).

Those two forces were pervasive inside West and, as such, shaped hiring strategies, career paths, the work environment, and much more. In that way, they indirectly (but systematically) determined the characteristics of the managerial population in the firm, and thus the capacity (or incapacity) of that population to provide effective leadership.

For example, because of the impact of those two forces, executives at West rarely had strong pre-West backgrounds or natural abilities. Stanton was an exception. Hiring managers, facing heavy pressure to contribute to an improvement in the firm's quarterly economic performance, usually looked for people who could do entry-level jobs with a minimum of training, for people who took direction well, and for the least expensive people available. For those managers, worrying about leadership capability and long-term leadership potential seemed like an unaffordable luxury. It never occurred to them, for example, to spend a lot of time and money visiting universities to look for people with potential. The firm did little to nothing to overcome that natural tendency. As a result, the hiring process almost never brought in people with top grades, nationally ranked achievers in sports, or unusually creative people. New hires with keen minds and strong interpersonal skills were very rare.

The management at West also tended to lack any number of skills and perspectives needed to provide effective leadership because their career experiences simply did not allow those assets to develop. Senior managers tended to be narrow, for example, because they came up through the organization via very narrow and vertical career paths, paths largely driven by short-term business pressures (it requires money for training and up-to-speed time when people are given horizontal moves) and parochial political pressures (managers don't want to give up their good people to other departments). Those narrow experiences rarely gave them the broad knowledge or the extensive set of relationships usually needed to provide effective leadership. The agendas those executives created, to cite another example, were often short-term, tactically oriented, and visionless, because the jobs they held for their first ten or twenty years at West demanded great attention to the short term and to tactical details, and little if any attention to anything else. Those jobs were usually a part of large, centralized, functional hierarchies that were held in place, once again, largely by short-term business pressures (such structures are "efficient" in a short-term sense) and parochial politics (it's hard to change them into smaller multifunctional units, because top functional executives often resist efforts to dismantle their fiefdoms).

Once again, West did little to overcome that pathological syndrome. The firm spent little money on training, and when quarterly earnings started to miss projections, the training budget was one of the first to go. People learned on the job, but what they learned, and how much, seems to have varied almost randomly. A person with little long-term leadership potential was just as likely to end up in a job with a lot of learning possibilities as a high-potential person. Little effort was expended to manage careers intelligently, to prevent people like Stanton from being abused by short-term crises, or to coach or provide feedback to those people. The firm also did little to retain the leadership talent it had. As a result, good people often gave up and went elsewhere, as Gerry did.

In other words, there seem to be some perfectly understandable reasons why West had a weak management which lacked the characteristics described in Exhibit 3–1—"Personal Requirements for Effective Leadership in Senior Management Jobs in Complex Organizations." An identifiable syndrome is involved, a syndrome driven by two very powerful forces that have traditionally overwhelmed (among other things) "programs" developed by the personnel department.

## THE HISTORY OF THE PROBLEM

To appreciate fully that pathological syndrome, one also needs to understand its history. As one would suspect, the problem did not just appear suddenly one day. An analysis of West's past shows that the syndrome had important roots, which go back to West's most successful years, when it dominated its markets and did not need much leadership capability to succeed. In that smaller and less complex company, a few really good top managers could provide sufficient leadership for the entire corporation. Finding, developing, and retaining those few managers was relatively easy, because the short-term business pressures were much less intense. In those circumstances, a combination of three practices worked quite adequately to staff important positions:

1. The attention of one senior executive, who personally made sure a few people with leadership potential were hired, developed, and retained
2. The internal promotions process, which let the people with the greatest leadership potential rise to the top
3. An occasional senior outside hire to make up for any gap between important job openings and internal candidates to fill those openings

Those three practices appear to have worked well at West until the firm became fairly large and complex, and until its markets became highly competitive. With the onset of size and complexity and competition, those practices (predictably) began to fail. One senior executive could no longer do it all. There were too many management jobs that required leadership, and far too many potential candidates for the watchful eye of a single person. Short-term pressures meant not enough "cream" was getting into the firm at the bottom, and some of that was being "curdled" on the way up (through experiences much like Stanton's). Increasing internal politics made outside hiring to make up the gap less likely, just as increased size and complexity made bringing in people successfully at senior levels more difficult.

So for historical reasons, West never developed the culture, systems, discipline, programs, and practices associated with creating sufficient leadership in a complex corporation facing considerable competition. Instead, it developed practices that worked well in an era of relative simplicity and market dominance, an era in which it needed only two or three executives who could provide effective leadership. When that era came to a close, those practices began to fail. But because business results, carried by the firm's historical momentum, deteriorated very slowly, the practices were not quickly replaced by a more appropriate set of approaches to attracting, developing, and retaining talent (amid defensive cries of "we don't need to change, we are doing just fine"). This led to a greater gap between the leadership the firm needed and the leadership its management was able to provide, which, in turn, led to more market erosion and other business problems that significantly increased short-term business pressures and parochial infighting. Because of those pressures, the people who got promoted increasingly were those who got short-term results, despite debilitating their organizations, and people who were politically astute. Those very people then had even greater difficulty than their predecessors in providing effective leadership in executive jobs. So a downward spiral developed.

By 1980, even though it was apparent to many people at West that their business problems were related to insufficient leadership, they found it most difficult to change the situation. Attempts to develop those executives who lacked some of the basic natural requirements for leadership rarely seemed to be successful (and there were so many of those people). Attempts to bring in large numbers of outsiders failed for many reasons (e.g., internal resistance and the difficulty of successfully getting senior-level outsiders to fit in, to mention but two). Attempts to change the basic practices that were creating these problems in the first place were usually overwhelmed by the short-term business pressures and parochial politics. And all of this was made even more difficult by the fact that a few of West's most senior managers did not try to help. Some rationalized that they could succeed, as they had in the past, with only a few people providing leadership. Others were too insecure to try to develop what they saw as potential rivals. So they protected their own perceived interests while employees, stockholders, customers, and suppliers suffered the consequences.

This is a sad case. And it is far from unique.

# CHAPTER 5

# Roots of the Problem: A Summary of Why Firms Like "West" Have Weak Managements

Although the details surrounding the West Products case are certainly idiosyncratic to West, the background studies completed for this book and evidence from a half dozen other sources[1] suggest that many of the fundamental patterns seen at West may be common to firms that have a very weak leadership capability in middle and senior management. Those patterns are summarized here in Exhibits 5–1 to 5–6, which deserve careful attention before proceeding on to Chapter 6.

Exhibit 5–1
*One Historical Syndrome Often Associated with Inadequate Leadership**

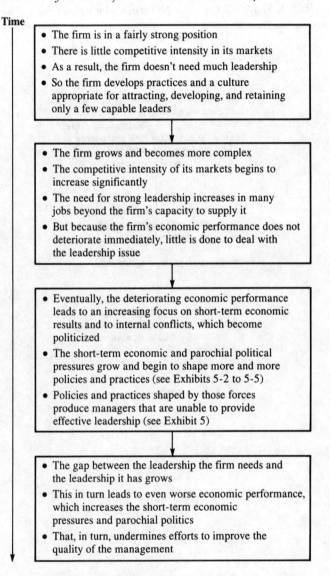

**Time**

- The firm is in a fairly strong position
- There is little competitive intensity in its markets
- As a result, the firm doesn't need much leadership
- So the firm develops practices and a culture appropriate for attracting, developing, and retaining only a few capable leaders

- The firm grows and becomes more complex
- The competitive intensity of its markets begins to increase significantly
- The need for strong leadership increases in many jobs beyond the firm's capacity to supply it
- But because the firm's economic performance does not deteriorate immediately, little is done to deal with the leadership issue

- Eventually, the deteriorating economic performance leads to an increasing focus on short-term economic results and to internal conflicts, which become politicized
- The short-term economic and parochial political pressures grow and begin to shape more and more policies and practices (see Exhibits 5-2 to 5-5)
- Policies and practices shaped by those forces produce managers that are unable to provide effective leadership (see Exhibit 5)

- The gap between the leadership the firm needs and the leadership it has grows
- This in turn leads to even worse economic performance, which increases the short-term economic pressures and parochial politics
- That, in turn, undermines efforts to improve the quality of the management

*This is not the only historical syndrome.

Exhibit 5–2
*How Short-Term Business Pressures and Parochial
Politics Shape the Quality of a Firm's Managerial Population*

Short-term business pressures
and parochial politics

↓

Hiring managers look for people who
require little training, will work for
minimum wages, and who take orders well.
They do not invest time and energy
looking for people with long-term
leadership potential.

↓

The employee base, from which people
are selected for promotions, is thin on
candidates with leadership
potential: keen minds, good
interpersonal skills, and high integrity.

↓

Management, made up mostly from
people in the employee base, lacks people
with some of the basic qualities needed
to provide effective leadership.

Exhibit 5–3
*A Second Example of How Two Powerful Forces*
*Shape the Quality of a Firm's Managerial Population*

Short-term business pressures
and parochial politics

↓

Bosses are very reluctant to give up
their good people. Impatient and
short-sighted young employees recognize that
the fastest way to the top is a straight
line. Bosses are reluctant to accept
lateral transfers who will require lots of
training, and who may not be good people.

↓

Career paths tend to be
very vertical and narrow.

↓

Most managers are narrow people,
who know others only in that part of the
organization where they grew up, and who have
a track records credible only to those people.

↓

Managers are unable to create the broad
agendas associated with effective leadership and have
difficulty gaining cooperation from the broad set of
players needed to provide real leadership.

Exhibit 5-4
*A Third Example of How Two Powerful Forces
Shape the Quality of a Firm's Managerial Population*

Short-term business
pressures and parochial politics

↓

The organizational structure
is functional and centralized (which is
both very efficient, in a short-term productivity sense,
and difficult to change because key functional
hands don't want to give up power). There is
lots of bureaucracy, because centralized
functional structures tend, over time,
to become very bureaucratic.

↓

People with management and leadership potential
spend their first ten to twenty years in very
tactical jobs. They do not get broad
assignments that deal with ambiguity
and strategy. They are not asked,
or allowed, to exercise
much leadership.

↓

Senior managers tend to be much better at operations and
tactics than at developing strategies.
Their agendas tend to be short-term-oriented
and to lack vision. They are much better
bureaucratic managers than leaders.

Exhibit 5-5
*A Fourth Example of How Two Powerful Forces*
*Shape the Quality of a Firm's Managerial Population*

Short-term business pressures
and parochial politics

↓

Strong pressures exist to bring really good people
into important jobs quickly. High
potentials manage their careers for
short-term personal gain.

↓

High potentials rise very
rapidly, staying in jobs a
very short time.

↓

Many senior managers have never had to live with
their past mistakes and learn from them. As a result,
they have not been able to develop really good business judgment
or the kind of interpersonal style that creates trust and
credibility over the long haul (i.e., not manipulative),
both of which are essential to effective leadership.
Their track records are also left somewhat ambiguous
because of their short tenures, and ambiguous
track records do not support the type of
credibility needed to provide
effective leadership.

Exhibit 5–6

*The Characteristics Needed to Provide Effective Leadership Versus
Characteristics Found Today in Firms Like "West Products"*

| | | Characteristics: What Is Needed | Characteristics: What Is Found |
|---|---|---|---|
| I. | Industry and organizational knowledge | Relatively broad knowledge of industry, business functions, & firm | Narrow/specialized knowledge of firm, functions, & industry |
| II. | Relationships within the firm and industry | Relatively broad set of good working relationships in the firm and industry | Good working relationships with (at best) the few subgroups of people with which they have worked |
| III. | Track record and reputation | Good track records and reputations in a relatively broad set of activities | Narrow track records that are credible to some but not to many others |
| IV. | Ability & skills | Keen minds and strong interpersonal skills | Mixed: Not uniformly strong at both the intellectual and interpersonal levels |
| V. | Personal values | High integrity: value all people and groups | Not uniformly high in integrity |
| VI. | Motivation | Strong desire to lead | Some desire to lead. Considerable desire to control |

# CHAPTER 6

# Assessing the Extent
# of the Problem: How Rare
# Is the "West" Case?

It is not difficult to find complaints about the lack of leadership in business today. It is very difficult, however, to evaluate their accuracy, the broadness of their applicability, or their accompanying theories of causality.[1]

The objective of this chapter is to try, despite the difficulties, to make a rough estimate of how common the syndrome described in the last two chapters is. More specifically, we shall attempt to determine how many firms are like West in the following four ways:

1. They have an inadequate management, because they do not attract and retain sufficient people with leadership potential in the first place, because they do not fully develop much of the potential possessed by the employees they do attract and retain, and because they fail to motivate (or allow) people to lead.
2. Their inability to attract, develop, retain, and motivate sufficient leadership potential can be traced to a multitude of inadequate practices: the way they handle college recruiting, the infrequency with which they move people across divisions and functions to broaden them, the lack of coaching and support from bosses, and much more.

63

3. Most inadequate practices are created by two very powerful forces that operate inside the firms—short-term economic pressures and parochial politics, forces which influence practices both directly by shaping managerial behavior and indirectly by influencing culture, structure, and systems.
4. The overall syndrome is a relatively new phenomenon, the product of a changing business environment, which is demanding more and more leadership, and the firm's inability (so far) to adapt successfully to that environment.

Each of those four points will be explored separately, beginning with the very first.

## ASSESSING HOW WELL FIRMS ATTRACT, DEVELOP, RETAIN, AND MOTIVATE LEADERSHIP TALENT

As a part of the background research conducted for this book, a questionnaire was developed which asks (among other things) how well firms attract, develop, retain, and motivate people who can provide effective leadership. A copy of this survey can be found in the Appendix.

The questionnaire was administered in two ways. In the first, it was given to executives attending company- or university-sponsored executive development training programs. In the second, a personnel officer gave it to a sample of executives (usually about thirty) in his or her firm.

Between July 1984 and December 1985, approximately nine hundred executives from more than one hundred firms filled out the questionnaire[2] (see Table 6-1 for a partial listing of the firms). Those people, with only a few exceptions, held the top 1 percent of jobs in their firms. In very large companies, they were usually among the top 0.5 or 0.25 percent of the total employee population. Such people were polled because they were in the best position to have the information needed to answer accurately the questions on the questionnaire about the quality of leadership within their own firms and about various practices that affect that factor.[3]

The questionnaire breaks the overall topic of leadership into three parts: (1) How well is the respondent's corporation doing with respect to attracting a sufficient number of people into the

Table 6-1
*A Partial Listing of the Firms That Employ Executives*
*Who Filled Out the Executive Resources Questionnaire*

| | |
|---|---|
| Allied/Signal | Intel |
| Bank of America | Marathon Oil |
| Barclays | Millipore |
| Bristol Myers | Mobil |
| Ciba-Geigy | NCR |
| Corning Glass | New York Life |
| Digital Equipment Corporation | Owens Illinois |
| Fairchild Aircraft | Phillips |
| General Electric | Sanders Associates |
| General Motors | The Sun Companies |
| Goodrich | 3M |
| GTE | |

firm who have the potential someday to provide effective leadership in important management jobs? (2) How well is it developing the potential of employees who might someday provide that leadership? (3) How well is it motivating and holding onto these people? Summary responses to those three questions are shown in Table 6-2.

Twenty-seven percent of the more than nine hundred executives polled said that their firms were doing a very good or excellent job of attracting a sufficient number of people with leadership potential. A slightly greater percentage (30 percent) said that their firms were doing a poor or fair job. Nineteen percent were optimistic (reporting very good or excellent) about how well their firms were developing employee potential. Fully 42 percent, more than twice as many, were pessimistic (reporting poor or fair) on that point. Approximately the same two-to-one pessimistic-to-optimistic ratio (43 to 20 percent) is also found on the question of retaining and motivating talent.

A literal interpretation of those results would be the following. The "average" senior executive filling out this survey believes his

Table 6–2
*Attracting, Developing, Retaining, and Motivating*
*Leadership Talent: Results from the Questionnaire*

---

I. How good a job is your company doing with respect to recruiting and hiring a sufficient number of people into the firm who have the potential some day of providing leadership in important management positions?

| | |
|---|---|
| % of Respondents Answering Very Good or Excellent | *27%* |
| % of Respondents Answering Poor or Fair | *30%* |

II. How good a job is your firm doing with respect to developing high-potential employees?

| | |
|---|---|
| % of Respondents Answering Very Good or Excellent | *19%* |
| % of Respondents Answering Poor or Fair | *42%* |

III. How good a job is your company doing with respect to retaining and motivating high-potential people?

| | |
|---|---|
| % of Respondents Answering Very Good or Excellent | *20%* |
| % of Respondents Answering Poor or Fair | *43%* |

---

or her firm does a better job than West Products of creating a leadership capacity in management. But the typical respondent does not describe his firm as doing a much better job in this regard. Indeed, it is a *rare* executive (one in four or five) who thinks his or her firm *is doing a very good job* overall of attracting, developing, retaining, and motivating enough people who can provide needed leadership.

If this were a poll of blue collar workers, the findings shown in Table 6–2 would probably surprise no one (except, perhaps, a few social cynics who would expect an even more negative assessment). What is interesting about the results, obviously, is that the people polled were senior executives in (more or less) respected corporations.

To help interpret further the results of the questionnaire, it is useful to look at two other recent large surveys that speak, at least to some degree, to the same issues. The first, conducted by Opinion Research Corporation, asked thousands of managers "How would you rate your company on the ability of top management?"[4] In the early 1970s, when the survey was first introduced, about 69 percent of those polled checked off "good" or "very good'' (the two best categories). By the early 1980s, that percentage had gone down to 47 percent. The second survey, done for *Fortune* in 1984, asked hundreds of outside experts to rate 250 corporations on a number of dimensions, one of which was a firm's ability ''to attract, develop, and keep talented people.''[5] Not one of the 250 firms received an excellent rating on this factor. Less than 7 percent got a very good rating. Fully 93 percent received a lower rating.[6]

One has to be cautious in interpreting this type of survey data for a long list of reasons.[7] Conservatively speaking, one might at least say that data from three large surveys suggest that the leadership problem at West Products, while probably not the norm in business today, is not that unusual.

That conclusion, although it will no doubt surprise some people, is entirely consistent with the discussion in Part I of this book. The information and analyses presented there strongly suggested that it would be difficult, on the dimension of leadership, for firms to adapt to some recent changes in the business environment. The evidence here supports that hypothesis.

## ASSESSING THE ADEQUACY OF CURRENT PRACTICES

The Executive Resources Questionnaire is particularly helpful in addressing the second question raised at the beginning of this chapter (regarding how many firms, like West, have difficulty with the leadership issue because of ''a multitude of inadequate practices''). The questionnaire lists forty-six practices (e.g., college recruiting efforts, compensation levels) that can affect a firm's ability to attract, develop, retain, and motivate a leadership capacity in management, and asks whether or not those practices are adequate today. Respondents rated each on a four-point scale: more than adequate, adequate, somewhat adequate, or inadequate. A summary of the responses to those questions is shown in Table 6-3.

Those results, no matter how one interprets them, are not very positive. Virtually no one (3.3 percent) thinks that the vast majority (80 percent) of the practices listed are adequate today in his or her firm. In fact, a majority of all the respondents found no less than 27 of 46 practices to be less than adequate (see Tables 6-4 and

Table 6–3
*Adequacy of Practices Affecting a Management's*
*Leadership Capacity: Results from the Questionnaire*

The questionnaire asks 46 questions about practices that affect the firm's capacity to attract, develop, retain, and motivate sufficient leadership. In summary form, here is how people responded:

   I. The vast majority of practices (80%) are more than adequate[a]
     % answering this way =     *0.2%*

  II. The vast majority of practices (80%) are adequate[b]
     % answering this way =     *3.3%*

 III. A bare majority of the practices (51%) are adequate[b]
     % answering this way =     *23.7%*

[a]A response of 1 on a 4-point scale (see the questionnaire).
[b]A response of 1 or 2 on a 4-point scale.

6–5). On a few items, as many as 80 or 90 percent of the executives polled reported that their firms' practices were not adequate!

For example, 82 percent of the executives who filled out the questionnaire reported that the quality of career planning discussions with bosses was less than adequate to support the objective of attracting and retaining a sufficient number of people who have the potential someday of providing effective leadership in important management positions in their firms. Seventy-seven percent said the developmental job opportunities available were also less than adequate to serve the same objective. Again, 77 percent said the same thing about "the information available to high potentials on job openings in the company."

Fully 93 percent of respondents reported that the way managers were rewarded for developing subordinates was less than adequate to support the need for spotting people with leadership potential, identifying their developmental needs, and then meeting those needs. In a similar vein, 89 percent of the executives said "the instruction given high-potential people regarding how to manage their own careers for long-term development" was less than adequate. Eighty-seven percent said the number and type of lateral transfers made for development purposes across divisions were also wanting. More than two-thirds of those polled also ques-

Table 6–4
*Programs and Practices Affecting the Firm's*
*Capacity to Attract, Retain, and Motivate Talent*

| Factors Affecting Attraction, Retention, and Motivation | *% of executives who felt the factor was less than adequate to support the objective of attracting, retaining, and motivating a sufficient number of people who have the potential of some-day providing effective leadership in important management positions* |
|---|---|
| 1. The quality of career planning discussions with bosses | 82% |
| 2. The developmental job opportunities available | 77% |
| 3. The information available to high potentials on job openings in the company | 77% |
| 4. Special programs offered to high-potential individuals | 68% |
| 5. Outside training opportunities | 65% |
| 6. The strategic/business and human resource planning processes which help clarify what kind of company will exist in 5–10 years, and thus how many and what kind of important management positions will need to be staffed then | 65% |
| 7. In-house training opportunities | 60% |
| 8. The capacity of hiring managers to identify and select high-potential people | 59% |
| 9. The promotion opportunities offered to high potentials | 56% |
| 10. The firm's incentive compensation plans | 52% |

Table 6–5
*Programs and Practices Affecting a Firm's
Capacity to Develop and Broaden Talented Employees*

| Factors Affecting Development | *% of executives who felt the factor was less than adequate to support the need for spotting high-potential people, identifying their developmental needs, and then meeting those needs* |
|---|---|
| 1. The way managers are rewarded for developing subordinates | 93% |
| 2. The instruction given high-potential people regarding how to manage their own career for long-term development | 89% |
| 3. The number and type of lateral transfers made for development purposes across divisions | 87% |
| 4. Special program aimed at identifying the development needs of high-potential people | 80% |
| 5. The number and type of lateral transfers made for development purposes inside divisions | 79% |
| 6. The mentoring, role modeling, and coaching provided | 79% |
| 7. The amount of carefully planned time and effort the company extends trying to manage the whole process of developing high-potential people | 79% |
| 8. The way special jobs are used to develop high-potential people | 77% |
| 9. The way feedback is given to subordinates regarding developmental process | 75% |
| 10. Special programs for spotting high-potential people | 72% |

| | |
|---|---|
| 11. The capacity of the firm's managers to identify the development needs of high-potential people | 70% |
| 12. The way responsibilities are added to the current jobs of high potentials for development purposes | 69% |
| 13. Formal succession planning reviews | 66% |
| 14. The firm's participation in outside management training programs | 65% |
| 15. The opportunities offered to people to give them exposure to higher levels of management | 60% |
| 16. The capacity of the firm's executives to identify people with potential | 57% |
| 17. The firm's use of in-company management training programs | 57% |

tioned the adequacy of lateral transfers inside divisions (across functions); the mentoring, role modeling, and coaching that are provided; the way feedback is given to people regarding their developmental progress; formal succession planning reviews; and still more (see Table 6–5).

Once again, a conservative interpretation of the data in Tables 6–3 to 6–5 would suggest that while the situation at West is probably not the norm in business today, it is not too far off center. Indeed, a literal interpretation of those tables says that *many* firms have *many* practices that are less than adequate to support the need to attract, retain, develop, and motivate a sufficient leadership capacity in management.

## ASSESSING THE FORCES BEHIND THE INADEQUATE PRACTICES

The Executive Resources Questionnaire does not address the third point raised at the beginning of this chapter (regarding how many firms, like West, have inadequate practices because of the overwhelming impact of short-term economic forces and parochial politics). But interviews conducted with a small sample of the people who filled out the questionnaire (about 8 percent) do provide some insight into this point. When asked in those interviews to talk about the inadequate practices they reported on the questionnaire, here is what people typically said:

> Until just this year, we offered no general management training opportunities to any of our middle or senior management. Not inside the firm, or at universities. None. We did sales training internally. And we sent MIS people to external technical courses. But any kind of training that didn't have an immediate payout—not us.

---

> We recently counted how many people in the past five years had been transferred into a different function or a different division in the firm for development purposes. That is, to help broaden the person for larger responsibilities. We found about twenty-five such moves, or five a year. That's in a company with 10,000 employees. Given how much bosses complain when you try to take a young person with potential away from them, I'm surprised that we have managed to move five a year.

---

> For people to develop, they need feedback. This is a basic principle of learning. The amount of good, solid feedback we give to our people is incredibly low. I personally know some very talented employees who have *never* been confronted with their weaknesses or developmental needs. Never. Their superiors just keep saying, "Good work, Jack, keep the old nose to the grindstone." And then we wonder why promising people often never blossom.

---

> Part of our problem is that our college recruiting efforts are inadequate. First of all, we hire people based on technical competence or potential in some specific area (e.g., accounting, MIS, market research, product engineering) with little or no emphasis on future managerial or leadership potential. This gets us people who can do entry-level jobs well, but not enough folks with long-term potential. And when you talk to our middle-level managers about this, they essentially say—"Give me a break. My job is to make my quarterly plan or budget. It is someone else's job to worry about that other stuff."

---

> The company I used to work for had an incredibly lackluster middle and upper-middle management. I obviously did not realize this when I joined them right out of college. But it didn't take long to

figure that out, or to figure out that that wasn't an accident, given the way people were managed and evaluated and promoted. I got the feeling after a while that this kind of management was exactly what the top five to ten officers wanted. They seemed to want obedient subordinates that weren't threatening in any serious way.

When interviewed, executives rarely say in an explicit way that inadequate practices were the product of "short-term economic forces" and "parochial politics." But, at the same time, implicit in almost all of their comments (as in those just quoted) is a concern about the impact of those two forces. A conservative interpretation: Short-term economic pressures and parochial politics clearly play some role in creating the inadequate practices that are often reported.

## ASSESSING THE HISTORY OF THE PROBLEM

Assessing the fourth aspect of the West situation—the history of this problem—is also obviously very difficult. Again, there are no relevant questionnaire data, but there is some information from those follow-up interviews.

The executives interviewed, who felt leadership was an important issue today, often talked about why they felt that way. Usually, they framed their remarks in historical terms. Here are some typical comments:

Our business environment has changed considerably in the last few decades. Technology is moving faster. The international competition is greater. The products have become much more complex.

I think a person who is successful today could have been successful ten or fifteen years ago, but not vice versa. Today we need broader people with a bit more competitive fire in the stomach. I wish I had more confidence that we were hiring and developing enough of these people.

---

We need a different kind of top management today than twenty years ago. Today we need people who really know their businesses, people who understand the product and the market. We need people who can take a long-term view of things, and who can help us to get lean, mean, and less bureaucratic. We need more of these people than we have on board right now.

---

Our business has gotten more competitive in the past decade, especially because of new foreign competition. The top team we now have—about 150 officers—would have been more than adequate to manage the business effectively twenty years ago. But today . . . I don't think more than sixty of them are really the kind of people we need. And I'm worried that things will get worse before they get better. Our officer jobs are getting tougher all the time, but our capacity to staff these jobs is not keeping up.

It is not at all unusual, when we have senior positions open, to have no internal candidate meet the job specs. None. I can't remember a time when we could actually choose among two or three fully qualified candidates, which is the way it should be, at least some of the time.

Historically, we never went to the outside to fill important management jobs. Now we are doing it all the time—too often, I'm afraid. Hiring so many outsiders is demoralizing our long-term employees. And the outsiders, at least half the time, aren't working out as well as expected.

---

We have traditionally had a superior team of senior executives—at least in our industry. But this is eroding swiftly because of the way our business is changing.

We have made two major acquisitions in the past few years. Within the next four years we will probably make one or more major acquisitions. All of these are outside our traditional businesses. We already have no one in senior management with experience in all our major businesses. And this problem will increase after the next acquisition. In five years, 80 percent of the key jobs will probably still be staffed by people who grew up in our old core businesses, despite the fact that they will represent only 30 percent of our revenues by then.

---

We have an excellent group of senior executives for running a highly regulated business. Unfortunately, we are no longer in a highly regulated industry.

---

Within ten years, the firm is going to be much more of a high-tech enterprise. But unless we do something very different, we will still have a low-tech senior management.

---

In the past we didn't need many leaders. But now, in a more competitive environment, we surely do. But what we have currently is a couple of good managers who can lead, a lot of very good managers who can't lead, and hordes of great administrators.

The bottom line in this case seems to be fairly straightforward: executives who feel leadership is an important subject today often seem to think the problem is a relatively new issue, the product of the kind of changing business environment described in Chapter 1.

## THE DATA: CONCLUDING COMMENTS

It is not possible to determine, with any precision, how common the problems identified in Chapters 4 and 5 are. But the information presented here clearly suggests that they are not at all rare. Indeed, one could easily draw the conclusion from the evidence in this chapter that the existence of enough effective leadership in management is the unusual situation today—that is, it is a rare firm that has successfully adapted to the changes in the business environment identified in Chapter 1.

This is a harsh conclusion, but it is entirely consistent with the analysis presented in Chapters 2 and 3. And it is obviously not inconsistent with the poor economic performance reported by many firms in the last few years (poor relative to the 1950s and 1960s).

The conclusion finds still further support when one examines the questionnaires and the interview notes from managers in firms with reputations for a much better than average leadership capacity today.[8] Even in those firms, one finds some concerns about insufficient leadership, inadequate practices, and the like, though the problems seem much less severe than in firms like West Products. An executive at Merck sums it up well:

> In today's increasingly complex and competitive business environment, we need all the strong leadership we can find, plus some. I personally think we do a much better job than most firms of finding and developing the right people. But we probably need to do an even better job in the future if we are going to continue to succeed as as a corporation. And, frankly, in some ways it is getting more and more difficult just to maintain our current level of success in this matter. This is a very tough issue. Very tough, and very important.

## PART III

# Creating a Leadership Capability in the Managerial Ranks

# CHAPTER 7

## Firms with a Superior Leadership Capacity:
Practices That Create Better-Than-Average Management Teams

It is not entirely clear whether there are any firms today that do a truly exceptional job of attracting, developing, retaining, and motivating leadership talent.[1] Nevertheless, some corporations clearly do achieve a level of success that is much superior (relatively) to others. Considerable evidence supports that conclusion—from the Executive Resources Questionnaire, the interviews done for this book, the *Fortune* Reputation Study, and elsewhere.[2]

If we are to improve current practice related to creating a leadership capacity within management groups and help firms break out of the syndrome seen in the West Products case, it would be useful to know what some corporations actually do to create those better-than-average management teams. That is the objective of Chapters 7 and 8.

## WHAT THE MANAGERIALLY STRONGER FIRMS DO DIFFERENTLY: EVIDENCE FROM THE QUESTIONNAIRE

A casual reading of management, leadership, and human resources literature can generate dozens of hypotheses regarding what is most important to creating a superior leadership capacity within management. Some writers imply that hiring standards are the key; bring in the right people, and everything else takes care of itself. Others focus on development; provide challenging job assignments to people early in their careers, and the leaders will emerge and grow. Some point to formal systems—succession planning, high-potential identification, or compensation reviews. Others suggest that more informal practices, such as the amount of mentoring and coaching provided, are key.

The Executive Resources Questionnaire provides one basis for testing those hypotheses.[3] The survey asks an overall question about the quality of a firm's management, as well as more specific questions about practices that affect that quality. Because there is a relatively broad range of responses to that first question (quality of management), we can see which (if any) of the more specific programs and practices seem to be associated with differences in that quality.

Tables 7–1 and 7–2 summarize the results of a very basic analysis of this sort. An examination of the first table shows that firms with superior managements are said to do a better job, on average, of attracting, developing, retaining, and motivating leadership talent (that is, *all four* aspects of the process). They achieve those results, the second table further suggests, by employing nothing less than dozens of more adequate practices.

More specifically, the detailed data (upon which Table 7–2 is based) say that those firms attract the people they need by having more adequate college recruiting efforts, programs for high potentials, training/educational opportunities, promotional opportunities, compensation, work environments, and reputations. They then hire the right people by having a more adequate sense of what

Table 7–1
*A Comparison of the "Stronger" Management Firms with All Others[a]*

|  | Stronger Management Firms | All Other Firms |
|---|---|---|
| 1. How good a job is the company doing with respect to recruiting and hiring a sufficient number of people into the firm who have the potential of someday providing effective leadership in important management positions? | 2.8 (1 = excellent, 5 = poor) | 3.4 |
| 2. How good a job is the company doing with respect to developing employees with potential? | 3.0 | 3.3 |
| 3. How good a job is the company doing with respect to retaining and motivating those employees? | 2.8 | 3.4 |

[a]Only firms in which twenty or more executives completed the questionnaire are included in this analysis. Firm scores are the simple mean of all the executives' responses. This and the next table compare the four firms scoring highest on item 57 (the "Stronger Management Firms") with fourteen lower-scoring firms.

they need to support business objectives, by keeping hiring standards high, and by having more hiring-level managers who can spot potential.

According to questionnaire data, those firms develop that talent by focusing scarce development resources on those who have the most potential. They spot that potential with more adequate performance appraisal processes, succession planning processes, and programs designed specifically to identify potential. They also tend to offer more opportunities to young people to get exposure to higher levels of management and have more executives at higher levels who can adequately spot young people with potential. They target development resources by more adequately identifying exactly what the development needs of those employees are. They then meet those needs in many ways, including adding responsibilities to jobs, creating special jobs, using inside and outside training, transferring people between functions and divisions,

Table 7–2
*A Comparison of Programs and Practices:*
*From the Executive Resources Questionnaire*

|  | Number of Areas in Which Stronger Firms Have: | | |
| --- | --- | --- | --- |
|  | *More Adequate Practices* | *Equally Adequate Practices* | *Less Adequate Practices* |
| 1. Regarding fifteen programs and practices that affect the recruitment and hiring of people with leadership potential | 14 | 1 | 0 |
| 2. Regarding nineteen programs and practices that affect the training and development of those people | 15 | 4 | 0 |
| 3. Regarding twelve programs and practices that affect the retention and motivation of such people | 12 | 0 | 0 |

mentoring and coaching employees, giving those people feedback on development progress, and giving them instruction in how to manage their own development.

Firms with better-than-average management retain and motivate the people they develop, according to questionnaire data, by having more adequate practices for them in the areas of compensation, promotion opportunities, development opportunities, and training opportunities. They also provide them with more adequate information on job openings in the firm and have higher-quality career planning discussions with them. And they offer those people a considerably better work environment.

*In other words, the questionnaire data suggest that no single program or small set of practices is key to creating a stronger-than-average leadership capacity within management.* Good succession planning, excellent college recruiting, or superior economic incentives, by themselves, appear not to be sufficient. The firms with better-than-average management seem to do a more adequate job in dozens of areas that affect the hiring, development, and retention of talent.

## WHAT FIFTEEN FIRMS DO DIFFERENTLY: EVIDENCE FROM THE "BEST PRACTICES STUDY"

That questionnaire-based conclusion receives further support with information from a second source: a more in-depth study of fifteen firms.

Those firms were chosen using data from *Fortune*'s Reputation Study.[4] The 1985 version of that survey asked hundreds of "experts" to rate 250 corporations on a number of dimensions, two of which were (1) the quality of the firms' management and (2) the firms' success at attracting, developing, and retaining talented employees. The twenty firms that were ranked the highest on those two dimensions are shown in Table 7–3. Fifteen of those firms were included in a "Best Practices" study as background for this book (the table identifies which fifteen). In using that procedure, it was not assumed that the fifteen firms had managements that were excellent in any absolute sense, nor that they had the best leadership capacity within their managements in a relative sense (relative to all other firms). It was assumed *only* that the fifteen represented a good sample of corporations with better-than-average managements.[5]

Eight or more top executives were interviewed in each of the fifteen firms, typically for an hour each.[6] The two core questions that structured the discussions were: (1) What do you do to attract and retain people with some leadership potential? (2) What do you do to develop and broaden those people?

The responses from the 150 interviews are entirely consistent with the questionnaire data. There are no big "secrets to success." These firms just do a lot of little things differently from the norm in business today. For our purposes here, a discussion of all the practices will be grouped into five sections relating to: a sophisticated recruiting effort, an attractive work environment, challenging opportunities, early identification, and planned development.

Table 7–3
*Firms Rated Highest on Two Dimensions[a]*
*in the 1985* Fortune *Reputation Study*

| Firm | Rating (1–10 Scale)[b] | Included in This Study |
|---|---|---|
| 1. IBM | 8.75 | Yes |
| 2. Dow Jones | 8.4 | Yes |
| 3. Hewlett-Packard | 8.4 | Yes |
| 4. Coca Cola | 8.35 | Yes |
| 5. Morgan Guaranty | 8.3 | Yes |
| 6. Anheuser-Busch | 8.3 | Yes |
| 7. 3M | 8.2 | Yes |
| 8. General Electric | 8.15 | Yes |
| 9. Boeing | 8.0 | No |
| 10. Citicorp | 7.9 | Yes |
| 11. Standard Oil of Indiana | 7.9 | No |
| 12. General Motors | 7.8 | Yes |
| 13. Du Pont | 7.75 | Yes |
| 14. Merck | 7.7 | Yes |
| 15. General Mills | 7.65 | Yes |
| 16. Johnson & Johnson | 7.6 | Yes |
| 17. Kodak | 7.55 | No |
| 18. Abbott | 7.55 | No |
| 19. Delta | 7.55 | No |
| 20. First Boston | 7.5 | Yes |

[a]"Quality of Management" and "Ability to Attract, Develop, and Keep Talented People."
[b]10 = excellent. Mean score on the two dimensions combined.

## A SOPHISTICATED RECRUITING EFFORT

Interviews from the "Best Practices" study suggest, first of all, that the fifteen firms do a superior job of recruiting sufficient people who have the potential of providing them with leadership at some time in the future. They do so by using a half-dozen practices that are slightly different from the norm today in business.

The first practice is to let line management drive the recruiting effort. At these firms, human resource professionals aid in the process, providing coordination and administrative support, but they do not seem to run the process. Line management does, including some fairly senior people. At General Mills, for example, even the chairman sometimes visits key colleges. At First Boston, the managing director who heads the recruiting effort literally spends half his time on recruiting. At Merck, the CEO himself devotes considerable time and effort to recruiting people who can help provide technical leadership in the firm. Although obviously expensive in terms of senior management time, most executives in these firms seem convinced it is necessary. A typical comment from one of those businessmen:

> Our current senior management is in the best position to know how many and what kind of people will be needed to run the business in the future; they understand where our business strategy is taking us better than anyone. They also are better able to spot the kind of quality minds and interpersonal abilities we want in young people; in a sense, it takes one to know one. And they are in a much better position to sell the company than are lower-level managers or personnel staff.

Second, many of these corporations target a limited number of colleges and universities that they feel are a good source of future leadership, and then they treat those schools much as they would major customers. Hewlett-Packard, for example, focuses on thirty schools for its corporate recruiting effort and works hard to develop good relationships with those schools by (among other things) networking with their faculties and donating computer equipment. When managed well, those efforts appear to pay off handsomely.[7]

Third, most of these firms seem to work especially hard to keep hiring standards high across the entire company. IBM, for example, quantifies certain measures of the quality of incoming hires, sets targets on those measures, and then "inspects" on a regular basis how well each hiring department is doing. Merck brings all high-potential recruiting candidates to corporate headquarters to meet some senior managers who are thought to have a good sense of the firm's hiring standards. General Mills does that too, and if any of those senior executives vote no on a candidate, they seriously consider not making an offer despite plenty of "yes" votes. Morgan Guaranty brings all new recruits to a lengthy training program in New York; if any of its offices are diluting hiring standards, it becomes rather obvious by the end of the program. The exact practices vary from firm to firm, but the main objective seems to remains the same: Keep standards from slipping because of short-term economic pressures.

A fourth practice that appears to distinguish most of these firms is that they actually pay some attention to leadership potential when recruiting. Morgan Guaranty, for example, asks everyone who interviews candidates to fill out a one-page "Prospective Employee—Interview Evaluation." The form gently reminds people to "keep in mind" four factors that have little to do with the technical components of banking; one of those factors is "leadership potential." "With all the well-educated and talented people we hire," an investment banker recently reported, "you'd think we would be guaranteed plenty of leadership and management potential. But it's not true. Unless we focus on that explicitly, we end up with a lot of smart technicians who often lack common sense and basic interpersonal skills."

A fifth practice commonly found at these firms might be called the well-managed "close." As one General Mills executive reported:

> When we find someone we really want, we work hard to close the sale. For example, if we meet such people at one of our informal wine and cheese gatherings, we'll immediately send a follow-up letter and invite them to Minneapolis. When they are here, we'll make sure they have lunch with a recent graduate of their school or someone from their home town. We will then make them an offer at the end of the day—no "We'll get back to you in a few weeks" stuff. Then, if they don't accept immediately, we might fly them and their spouses back to corporate to see the community and meet the chairman. In between, there will be all the appropriate follow-up letters and calls.

Finally, these firms usually evaluate their overall recruiting at least once a year. Many generate statistics on offers made to offers accepted, or offers lost to key competitors, and then compare those statistics to historical averages. Some, like Du Pont, look at more indirect indices, such as how many relatively new hires are rated on the yearly performance appraisal as having high potential.

## AN ATTRACTIVE WORK ENVIRONMENT

A few years ago I visited a former student who works for Hewlett-Packard. By job standards, he was doing very well at the time. At age thirty-four, he was in charge of hundreds of people and a sizable budget. But by salary standards, he was making 25 percent less than the average person who graduated in his MBA class. When I questioned him about this, he admitted that he wished he made more money. He also volunteered that he had considered on several occasions leaving HP for start-up ventures. But he hadn't. I asked why.

The long answer the young man provided basically boiled down to this: Hewlett-Packard has been a good place for a talented person to work. People are treated well. Competence is respected. Bureaucracy and political games are minimized. Individual initiative is recognized and rewarded. It is technically a very exciting place for people with engineering backgrounds, etc., etc.

What is so interesting about that response is that it is not at all unusual at the fifteen "Best Practices" firms. When one asks executives at those firms how they attract and retain good people, almost always they say "because it's a great place to work." Why they think it's a great place to work seems to vary somewhat from firm to firm and from individual to individual. What remains constant is their belief that it's "fun" for someone with leadership potential to work there.

Perhaps the most common answer regarding what makes a work environment fun is "lack of politics." By that, people typically mean the environment is friendly. ("When someone gets the knife out around here it is made of rubber.") They also mean that results are what count, not covert alliances or form. And they mean that people actually try to help each other. "I could get a job at (another prestigious newspaper)," a Dow Jones manager says, "but I'm not interested. Politics here are 10 percent of what they are over there. We don't have their warring factions. I mean, who wants to have to put up with that? It's not worth it."

Executives also often mention honesty or integrity as an important feature of a good work environment. Johnson & Johnson people, for example, often refer to the fact that they usually live up to the high ethical standards outlined in their "CREDO," and that makes J&J's environment very attractive. Executives at other firms sometimes talk about other corporate values, such as a dedication to quality (one hears that often at Dow Jones and Anheuser-Busch). They talk about the lack of bureaucracy or the informality. They talk about the quality of their fellow workers. They sometimes refer to the nice location of the workplace (e.g., 3M in Minneapolis, Coke in Atlanta) or the aesthetics of the work environment (Morgan Guaranty). And they often point out that "people are treated well around here."

For example, one of the frequent complaints one hears from lower-level managers in many firms is that they feel "trapped." Here is a very typical comment:

> I have almost no idea what job openings exist or will exist outside my department. That kind of information just doesn't circulate at my level. So my capacity to get a good opportunity in some other part of the company is almost completely under the control of my bosses. Unfortunately, they don't have much incentive to want to find those opportunities for me. So I'm trapped in a narrow and vertical career path, which in the long run won't be good for me. And the speed of my movement on this path is a function of strong forces I don't control. It's not a good situation. It's driving me to look for opportunities outside the company.

The fifteen firms studied here seem to do a much better job than average of minimizing that problem by providing high potentials (and often others too) with information on job openings throughout the company. Hewlett-Packard, for example, has worked to maintain a labor market inside the company that is at least as open and accessible as external markets. Most people really appreciate those efforts, and such practices facilitate lateral movement for development purposes (more on that later).


CHALLENGING OPPORTUNITIES

Interviews at the fifteen "Best Practices" firms are replete with references to the importance of "challenging opportunities." One gets the sense that challenging entry-level jobs help attract good people in the first place, and challenging promotion opportunities help firms hold onto those people, because people with leadership potential love new challenges and hate old routines. The challenges, in turn, both stretch people and allow them, often early in their careers, to exercise some leadership. And that, of course, is at the heart of development.

Those interviewed say that challenging opportunities are created in a number of ways. In many firms, decentralization is the key. By definition, decentralization pushes responsibility lower in an organization and in the process creates more challenging jobs at lower levels. Johnson & Johnson, 3M, HP, General Electric, and a number of other well-known firms have used that approach quite successfully in the past.

Some of those same firms also have created as many small units as possible so there are lots of challenging little general management jobs available. Hewlett-Packard, GE, and J&J are said to have benefited greatly over the years from that approach.

In a similar vein, many of the firms seem to develop additional challenging opportunities by stressing growth through new products: 3M has even had a policy over the years that at least 25 percent of its revenue should come from products introduced within the last five years. That encourages small new ventures, which in turn offer hundreds of opportunities to test and stretch young people with leadership potential.

Some of those same firms have also worked hard to minimize bureaucracy and rigid structures so that it's easier to enhance jobs with additional challenges. As an executive at Coca Cola recently put it:

> If I hire an MBA as a brand manager, because we are not highly compartmentalized and structured, he or she can make that job into almost anything. The person is not in a box. We can make the job as big and challenging as is necessary to really turn that person on.

In a similar way, more and more companies, like Du Pont, seem to be using task force assignments to generate additional challenge in jobs.

Other firms, including some that face limits to how much they can decentralize responsibility into small units, have created specific jobs to challenge people with leadership potential. Perhaps the most obvious example is administrative assistant (or executive assistant) jobs. Anheuser-Busch has created about thirty such jobs. IBM has even more, and has obviously benefited from the practice. The last few presidents and many of the current executive staff at IBM had AA jobs early in their careers.

When all of those techniques still do not produce enough opportunities, perhaps because the business (or part of the business) is not growing, these firms then (more often than the norm in business today) take the painful actions needed to free up promotion possibilities. That sometimes means making early retirement attractive to certain people. And it always means coming to grips with "blockers"—people who have no chance of further promotion, are a long way from retirement, and are not performing well in their current assignments.

## EARLY IDENTIFICATION

Equipping people with what they will need to provide effective leadership takes time, often lots of time. As such, it is not entirely surprising to find that the fifteen firms seem to do a far better job than average of identifying people with some leadership potential early in their careers and identifying just what will be needed to stretch and develop that potential.

The methods most of those firms use are surprisingly straightforward. They go out of their way to make young employees and people at lower levels in their organizations visible to senior management. Senior managers then judge for themselves who has potential and what the development needs of those people are. Executives then discuss their tentative conclusions openly and candidly, among themselves, in an effort to draw more and more accurate judgments. "Scientific" techniques seem to be rarely employed. The key is: look, talk, and think.

To make younger employees visible to senior management, a variety to techniques are said to be utilized. Here are the most common, each described by an executive whose firm uses that approach:

> We regularly take young people who someone thinks has potential and put them on special projects that conclude with presentations to senior management. I can still remember making a presentation

when I was thirty years old to a group that included the chairman of the company.
*An executive at Johnson & Johnson*

Once a month, I have a luncheon with one of my key functional managers, and I always ask that he or she bring some high-potential employees along. At certain staff meetings, I do the same thing. This allows me to get to know a lot of young people and to draw my own conclusions about potential, strengths, and weaknesses.
*An executive at Coca Cola*

We don't let the organizational structure constrain us. We always go right to the individual who has information we need. This puts us in contact with a lot of lower-level and more junior employees, and gives us a firsthand feeling for who they are and what they are good at.
*An executive at Dow Jones*

We have many recognition programs in this company. These programs often bring good people to the attention of senior management. They make good people more visible, which is very helpful.
*An executive at General Mills*

One of the things we do is to set up situations which allow our divisions to put there best people "on stage." And then we take a hard look. In this way, you can spot promising young people, and once you know their names, you can go out of your way to get to know them better.
*An executive at Hewlett-Packard*

Our top people make it a habit to get out to our plants on a regular basis. This gives them a chance to meet and to talk to younger employees. It makes folks visible to senior executives who would never meet them otherwise.
*An executive at Anheuser-Busch*

Those kinds of practices provide senior managers with information on people who might have leadership potential. Those executives then usually share and discuss that information among themselves, either informally or formally, on a regular basis.

The Management Council at Hewlett-Packard (the top twenty-eight people), for example, has had regular discussions about the middle management at the company, and the discussions are reported to be "very open." Large firms tend to try to do that sort of thing in a very systematic way. At Du Pont, for example, the sixteen senior department heads meet once a month for two hours. At a typical meeting, the agenda will include a discussion of the half-dozen people one of those executives thinks are "highly promotable." Before every meeting, a picture and biography for those six people are sent to all sixteen department heads. At the meeting, everyone who knows those people is expected to speak up, especially those who have concerns or questions about a person's potential (e.g., "When Harry worked for us five years ago, he only performed at an average level. What has happened to him recently that led you to think so highly of him?"). People who don't know the candidate being discussed are also expected to be aggressive in their questioning (e.g., "How does she compare to George Smith?" "How well did he do in his one staff assignment?").

## PLANNED DEVELOPMENT

Armed with a better-than-average sense of who has some leadership potential and what needs to be developed in those people, executives in the "Best Practices" firms then spend much more time than firms like West Products planning for that development. Sometimes that is done as a part of a formal succession planning or high-potential development process. Often it is done more informally. In either case, the key ingredient appears to be an intelligent assessment of what feasible development opportunities fit each candidate's needs.

"Developmental opportunities," in the sense that the term is being used here, include:

- New job assignments (promotions and lateral moves)
- Formal training (inside the firm, at a public seminar, or at a university)
- Task force or committee assignments
- Mentoring or coaching from a senior executive
- Attendance at meetings outside one's core responsibility
- Special projects
- Special developmental jobs (e.g., executive assistant jobs)

With the fifteen firms studied here, one finds those opportunities used more systematically than is the norm in business today. One finds (as this writer did) a Ph.D. organic chemist (at Coke) working as an executive's administrative assistant as part of a conscious strategy to broaden that person. One finds bankers (in Morgan and Citicorp) or functional heads (at J&J) systematically shipped off to foreign offices to give them international experience and a chance to run a small operation by themselves. One finds technically trained people (at Du Pont) moved from research to manufacturing to marketing to general management to corporate staff, and then into executive line jobs. One finds people (at IBM) regularly attending some type of educational experience. One finds, again and again, what appears to be considerable intelligent effort being expended to develop and broaden people so that they will someday have what it takes to provide leadership in complex executive jobs.

One also finds some effort in these firms not just to plan for development in a generic sense, but to plan for the kind of development that will support future business strategies. Sometimes that is done very formally (e.g., strategic business planning is somehow tied to succession planning). Often it is more informal. It is not clear how effective those efforts are, but some executives clearly think they are important.

And when formal training is used—and it seems to be used a great deal in these firms—it is never employed as a substitute for experience. Unlike in firms like West Products, where training is often used as a "quick fix,"[8] in these firms training both leverages past experiences (that is, it helps people to learn more from them) and prepares people to learn more from future assignments (in making them more aware of certain things).[9]

## THE FINDINGS IN PERSPECTIVE

The findings in this chapter are consistent with Peters and Waterman's[10] notion that sucessful firms do a lot of little things a little better, as well as the Center for Creative Leadership work[11] on how effective executives are developed. Even more fundamentally, in light of the discussion in Chapters 1, 2, and 3, these findings have a certain logic to them. The business environment today is asking many people to help provide leadership. Doing that effectively is often extremely difficult. Indeed, the assets one needs to provide effective leadership in big jobs form a long list (remember

Exhibit 3-1: "Some of the Personnel Requirements for Effective Leadership in Senior Management Jobs in Complex Business Settings"). Trying to find and equip many people with the tools they will need to provide that leadership might therefore logically be a large and very complicated task, one that should require a great effort in a lot of different areas. And that is essentially what the evidence in this chapter says (the relationship of the practices identified in this chapter to the requirements shown in Exhibit 3-1 is summarized in Exhibit 7-1).

To put the magnitude of the task in perspective, let us remember that it seems to take all of this effort to produce what we have been calling "better-than-average" managements. That is, we have no evidence to suggest that any of the firms in the "Best Practices" study have managements that are, at least on the leadership dimension, excellent in any absolute sense. These firms simply have managements that are better able to supply leadership in competitively intense industries than is the norm today in business. Just imagine what might be required to produce truly excellent managements.

Exhibit 7-1
*How Practices Create a Leadership Capacity in Management*

*Practices Found in Firms with Better-than-Average Managements*

*Impact on the Personal Requirements for Effective Leadership (from Exhibit 3-1)*

1. A sophisticated recruiting effort

2. An attractive work environment

Helps bring in enough people with basic leadership potential—that is, with integrity, intelligence, empathy, energy, and some drive to lead

3. Challenging Opportunities

Helps retain and motivate enough of these people

4. Early identification (of potential and development needs)

5. Planned development

Helps develop in people a broad understanding of the industry and organization, a broad set of good working relationships, excellent track records and reputations, as well as some higher-level intellectual and interpersonal skills.

# CHAPTER 8

# The Forces Behind the Practices:

## What It Takes to Mitigate Short-Term Economic Pressures and Parochial Politics

A first step in understanding why some firms have better managements than others is to identify what those firms do differently that helps them attract, develop, retain, and motivate a superior leadership capability. Although obviously necessary, that step is not, however, sufficient. One also needs to understand why firms like those described in the last chapter are able to do what they do. More specifically, why are they not overwhelmed by the short-term economic pressures and parochial politics that seem to drive events in some organizations today? How do they avoid the syndrome summarized in Chapter 5?

Providing some answers to those most important questions is the purpose of this chapter.[1]

## THE ROLE OF LINE MANAGEMENT

At one level, the descriptions given in Chapter 7 already provide one answer to the questions just posed. That answer goes something like this: When one finds the kinds of practices described in the last chapter, one also tends to find a line organization that assumes some responsibility for making those practices a reality and that works to achieve that objective. Line management does not delegate that responsibility to the personnel staff (as seems to happen in so many firms). Nor do they abdicate any and all responsibility (which is what happens in firms like West Products).

That simple fact appears to be of enormous importance. Because of the magnitude of competitive intensity and organizational complexity found today, short-term economic pressures and parochial politics probably lurk everywhere. Unleashed, they become very powerful forces. Keeping them in check should logically require a countervailing force of great power. A personnel program for leadership development or the good intentions of a few people does not constitute such a force. The collective will of the line organization does.

Some of the ways this sense of responsibility manifests itself are quite visible. Many managers in firms with superior management are said to spend more time in meetings directly related to this topic than do their counterparts elsewhere. But some ways are more subtle. Managers at those firms seem to spend more time, *as a regular part of the management process*, looking for signs of potential in employees, looking for ways to develop people, and encouraging subordinates to manage their own career development in an intelligent way. Informal corridor and premeeting conversations at those firms more frequently deal, if only for a few moments, with issues related to recruiting, developing, and retaining a leadership capacity. And much more often one finds, in conversations that are officially about markets, products, or technology, an implicit concern about people and their development, retention, and motivation.

For example, here is part of an actual conversation that took place recently at a firm with a reputation for better-than-average management.[2] The managers involved are a division president and one of his sales executives. The topic, however, is not this month's (or this week's) orders versus the sales plan. The topic of conversation is a talented young employee:

GENERAL
MANAGER:    How is Karen doing these days? (Karen had been iden-
            tified as a young district sales manager with much
            future potential.)

| SALES | |
|---|---|
| MANAGER: | Very well, although I'm scared we are going to lose her someday soon. |
| GM: | Why? |
| SM: | Our competitors know of her because she has a visible job, and some of them I'm sure are trying to lure her away. |
| GM: | So what are we doing to try to keep her? |
| SM: | Well, we're doing everything we can. But there are limits, you know. In about one year she is going to be wanting a promotion to regional sales manager, and I don't have any regional jobs to give her. |
| GM: | Will she be able to handle a regional sales manager job in a year? |
| SM: | I think so. |
| GM: | So why won't we be able to offer her one? |
| SM: | They are all taken, and none of those guys are moving on again in the near future. |
| GM: | And you know as well as I why that is. Your predecessor had a tendency to promote the best salesperson to district sales manager, regardless of lack of managerial or leadership potential. Then some of these people got pushed up into regional manager jobs. None of them are doing an exceptional job. And if we don't do something, they will sit in those jobs forever. |
| SM: | True, but what do we do about it? None of them is failing. I don't see that it is fair to fire any of them. |
| GM: | I'll tell you what we can do. We need to sit down and talk to George, who is probably the biggest misfit in that kind of job. We need to confront him with the facts about his performance, and explore lateral moves out of your group or even a demotion in the group. We can keep his salary fixed, so as not to put a hardship on his family. But we have to face up to the issue, for Karen's sake, and for others like her. |

That kind of conversation—which, by the way, took only about seventy seconds—is rarely heard in some corporations. In firms where it does occur, one gets the sense that line managers, from the CEO all the way down to supervisors, make it happen.

## THE ROLE OF CULTURE

Taking the analysis one more step, one would ask: But what creates this kind of will and shared sense of responsibility among line managers? Why don't they ignore the leadership issue or delegate it to their staff, as happens in many firms?

When interviewing managers for the "Best Practices Study" as background for the book, this writer repeatedly asked *why* managers in those firms behaved the way they did, and why the firms did not seem to suffer the syndrome described in Chapter 5 and exemplified by "West Products." "You say that you broaden employees via lateral moves, but why don't you run into the problem of managers hoarding their best young people and not allowing them to move laterally? Many firms seem unable to produce intelligent lateral movement. Why do managers here behave differently?"

When asked those questions, people usually stared into space for a few moments and then replied: "That's just the way we are" or "That's just the way we do things around here." In other words, they said that it is somehow built into the very culture of their corporations.

Almost all of the "Best Practices" firms seem to have moderately strong corporate cultures, which are almost clannish in nature and place a high value on doing what is necessary to make the firm prosper over the long term. Those cultures are characterized by norms that are very supportive of the kinds of practices described in the last chapter and push people to downplay short-term economic pressures and parochial political forces.

Here are four actual responses to the question, "Why don't you suffer the problems found in companies like [West Products]?":

First of all, we feel that we have an obligation to broaden and stretch people. That's just the way we are. People that don't think that way—people low in integrity that are just out for themselves, for example—don't do well around here.

We try to take risks with people to stretch them. We don't mind giving people a little rope, even early in their careers here. The culture supports risk-taking. And if it doesn't work out, we don't shoot people.

The environment here is also pretty open and family-like. As such, it's relatively easy to move people across departments or divisions for development purposes. And young people feel comfortable, in this environment, to go talk to senior people outside their immediate groups about possible future job opportunities.

We know our culture has helped us to prosper in the past and we are trying to consciously maintain and renew it. For example, in April of 1986, our top 130 officers got a package of videotapes and materials that were designed to help them hold "Cultural Renewal" meetings with their people. These materials list twelve aspects of our traditional culture and asks them to discuss whether each is still relevant and feasible to maintain today. The materials included a video of our top three officers talking about all this.

*An executive at 3M*

Managers around here wouldn't think of trying to hire second-class people. Trying to find the best is too deeply imbedded in the fabric of the place. Senior executives ask questions. If a unit doesn't hire good people, they will find that out.

Also, after you have been here a while, you learn that in order to succeed, you have got to hire and develop good people. I can think of a couple of very talented managers who haven't done well here. Part of their problem was that they didn't create a strong staff underneath them. They didn't go out and get good people and then broaden them, which is the way you do things around here.

*An executive at Citicorp*

You want to know why we keep our hiring standards high, why we encourage people to go to seminars to develop themselves, and the like? We do it because our culture encourages this sort of thing. It emphasizes quality in everything, including our staff and management.

*An executive at Anheuser-Busch*

Our team-oriented culture simply doesn't allow people to play political games like hiding their good, young employees. People gang up against someone like that. It also makes lateral transfers for development relatively easy to produce. We value broad-based people and have a tradition of sorts of producing them.

*An executive at Morgan Guaranty*

Why do we do all these things? I guess we have historically valued managers who could hire good people and then bring them along. So we just encourage that behavior in all our managers. That's it. Period.

*An executive at Hewlett-Packard*

A strong culture is a very powerful force.[3] In an environment where potent short-term economic pressures and parochial politics can easily come to rule behavior, just such a force may be necessary to keep line management focused on any centrally important corporate objective. And that is what we seem to find in firms with superior managements.


THE ROLE OF STRUCTURE, SYSTEMS, AND POLICY

Although culture seems to be the key force in getting line managers to create the kinds of practices described in the last chapter, formal structures, policy, and systems do play some role in shaping behavior, especially in very large firms.

For example, virtually no firms that have reputations for superior managements are both highly centralized and highly bureaucratic. Even those that lean in one or both directions seem to be working hard today to get rid of unnecessary bureaucracy and to decentralize more. The reason is probably related to one simple fact: A very centralized structure and a set of highly bureaucratic systems do not support many of the practices described in the last chapter. They make it difficult, for example, to offer young people with potential challenging opportunities and leadership possibilities early in their careers. Conversely, a relatively decentralized structure and moderately unbureaucratic systems make it easier to produce those opportunities in large numbers.

That is not to say that firms with superior leadership have no bureaucracy. The big ones probably all do, including some aimed specifically at encouraging the practices described in Chapter 7. A good example, described later in this chapter, is the process of creating candidate "slates." A more common example would be formal succession planning systems.

The largest of the fifteen "Best Practices" firms also tend to have some (more or less) formal policy designed to support sound development practices. A good example is shown in Exhibit 8-1. Listed there are ten policies for management development created at GE at some time in the mid-1970s.

It is fairly obvious how these policies help support the development of a leadership capacity in management. For example, the very first two points state, about as explicitly as possible, who is responsible for creating the next generation of management (the

Exhibit 8-1
*GE's Management Development Philosophy: Circa 1975*

1. ASSURING DEVELOPMENT OF MANAGERIAL EXCELLENCE IN THE COMPANY IS THE CHIEF EXECUTIVE'S MOST IMPORTANT RESPONSIBILITY.

2. MANAGERS AT ALL LAYERS MUST BE SIMILARLY RESPONSIBLE AND MUST "OWN" THE DEVELOPMENT SYSTEM(S).

3. PROMOTION FROM WITHIN—FOR ITS MOTIVATIONAL VALUE—WILL BE THE RULE, NOT THE EXCEPTION.

4. A KEY STEP IN PLANNING THE DEVELOPMENT OF MANAGERS IS THE MANPOWER REVIEW PROCESS.

5. MANAGERIAL ABILITIES ARE LEARNED PRIMARILY BY MANAGING. OTHER ACTIVITIES ARE VALUABLE ADJUNCTS.

6. CONTROL OF THE SELECTION PROCESS IS ESSENTIAL IN ORDER TO USE OPENINGS DEVELOPMENTALLY.

7. THE COMPANY CAN TOLERATE AND NEEDS A WIDE VARIETY OF MANAGERIAL STYLES, TRAITS, ABILITIES, ETC.

8. SEVERAL DIFFERENT MANAGERIAL STREAMS AND DEVELOPMENT PLANNING SYSTEMS ARE NEEDED TO ACCOMMODATE THE COMPANY'S SIZE, DIVERSITY, AND DECENTRALIZATION.

9. OCCASIONALLY, IT MAY BE NECESSARY TO DISTORT OTHERWISE SOUND COMPENSATION PRACTICE AND/OR TO CHANGE ORGANIZATIONAL STRUCTURE TO ACHIEVE DEVELOPMENTAL RESULTS.

10. STAFF PEOPLE MUST ADD VALUE IN THESE PROCESSES, BUT THEIR ROLES ARE SECONDARY TO THE MANAGERIAL ROLES.

CEO and line management). If any additional ambiguity exists on that point, it is eliminated by Point 10 ("The staff" must "add value . . . but their roles are secondary to the managerial roles"). Note that fully three of ten policy statements are used to make that centrally important point clear.

Point 3 says that management will not be bought in large numbers in the outside labor market, but must be developed from within. If that doesn't happen, the policy reminds us, it will be increasingly difficult to attract, retain, and motivate young people with leadership potential, because giving away challenging promotional opportunities to outsiders on a regular basis is demoralizing.[4]

The fourth point talks about the importance of a "manpower review process." In such a review, the entire line organization is asked periodically to pause and take a hard look at their people, especially people with potential to staff important managerial jobs. The system asks them to think about questions like: Whom do we have with potential? How far can these people go? Are there enough of these people? If not, why not? For each one, what is his or her developmental needs? What did we do in the last six to twelve months to work on their needs? How successful were we? How can we realistically make some more progress in the next six months, one year, or two years in meeting those needs?

GE's fifth policy is particularly interesting in light of how much money it spends on training. It has a permanent management development center in Ossining, New York. It spends much time and effort training managers. But at the same time, it clearly states that formal training is only "a valuable adjunct" to the primary mechanism for learning. And that, of course, is experience on the job.[5]

The sixth point is impossible to understand from the statement itself ("control of the selection process is essential in order to use openings developmentally"). The belief behind the policy can be summarized as follows: Because of short-term business pressures and parochial political pressures, if a firm does not exercise some "control" over how managers select people when they have a job opening, sufficient job openings will not be used for development purposes.

At GE, control has been exercised in the following way. If you were a department manager or higher, when you had a job opening, policy has required that you first call the appropriate personnel person. He or she would work out a job description with you and then ask you two questions: (1) Do you know anyone who can do the job well? (2) Do you know anyone for whom the job would be a good developmental assignment? After you have provided that input, the personnel person would ask similar questions of your boss, your boss's boss, personnel people in other parts of the business, perhaps even some of your peers. He or she would then develop a single list or "slate" of candidates. If it was long, it would be shortened by the appropriate people (like your boss). Finally the slate would be given to you, and then you would have the right to interview those people (*only*) and to choose one. The slate would usually contain one or more candidates put on the list for development programs. And if one of those missing from the list is the person who jumps to attention whenever you enter a room because you promised him the job, that's too bad. He's out.[6]

Points 7 and 8 are related. The first says that "the company can tolerate and needs a wide variety of managerial styles, traits, abilities, etc." The second says "Several different managerial streams and development planning streams are needed to accommodate the company's size, diversity, and decentralization." Those policies probably exist to counteract a natural tendency to make the processes associated with management development too centralized and homogeneous (the so-called cookie-cutter syndrome). In a large firm that operates in many markets, with many products, employing many technologies, too much homogeneity can be deadly over the long run.

Finally, point 9 says "Occasionally it may be necessary to distort otherwise sound compensation practices and/or to change organizational structures to achieve development results." In other words, sometimes to make a lateral developmental move work, one needs to pay someone more than the regular pay for that position to help encourage the person to take the job (which might have a pay grade less than his or her current job). Occasionally it might be necessary to add positions to the structure or organize in some way that is not needed to achieve today's business results, in order to create a developmental position for someone. In either case, policy explicitly supports doing what is needed to develop effective managers.

## THE ROLE OF THE CEO

The line is key, and in firms with superior managements both corporate culture and formal systems seem to encourage line managers to do the right thing. But there is still one or more element that appears to be very important here, an element that helps shape the behavior of line managers directly and also influences that behavior indirectly through its impact on corporate culture and formal systems. That element is the CEO.[7]

A decade ago studies were conducted at both IBM and GE, quite independently, of how their CEOs actually allocated their scarcest resource—their own time. In each case, a long list of fifty or so possibilities was developed, one of which relates to the topic of this book. In each case, a procedure was developed to keep track of the issues the CEO chose to deal with day after day for a few months.

At a recent gathering of senior executives, this writer asked the audience how high they thought the item related to "attracting, developing, retaining, and motivating a management that can provide leadership" could place—realistically, not ideally or theoretically—for a real live CEO? After a cynical reply of "fifty-first place out of fifty" one person said, "maybe as high as fifth place." All those around him at the time laughed out loud! That very typical response makes the results of the experiment at GE and IBM all the more remarkable, because at those two firms an item similar to that is said to have placed FIRST!

An IBM executive once told this writer: "Of all the factors we control which can affect our future prosperity, many of us think two are particularly important. They are technology and leadership. In terms of the priority of the two, it becomes clear when we look at our own history. Looking back, it is hard to find instances where technology produced managers who could lead. But it is easy to find instances in which good leadership produced good technology. So leadership should be our number one priority, especially the CEO's."

There are dozens of stories about how Watson, Carey, and Opel—some of the executives most responsible for IBM's incredible success in the 1950s, 1960s, and 1970s—made the leadership factor a priority. It is not certain that any of the stories are actually true. The mere fact that they are believed and told again and again is probably even more important than whether or not they actually happened.[8] For example, in one story, one of the former IBM CEOs cuts off a meeting ten minutes early with a division president (someone running a multibillion-dollar business) and says something like, "Fred, let's change the subject for a moment. It's August now, and you've got this year's group of college grads on board. Would you tell me who you think are the ten best people your division hired from college this year, why you think they're the best, and what kind of jobs we have them in?"

In another story, the CEO allegedly looks a division president in the eye and says, "Charlie, I see that six high-potential young people from other divisions moved into your division this year and not one of your best high potentials moved out. How can we develop general managers if we keep doing that? Listen, I'd appreciate your doing the following for me. Come back in three weeks with a comprehensive plan for cross-functional and inter-site development for ten of your best people. We'll discuss the plan, and then a year from now, we will revisit the issue and see how well you did.''

At GE, Reg Jones, the former CEO, gave leadership a priority by, among other things, the way he handled his own succession. Jones began the process years before his scheduled retirement. Working with his board and the head of Executive Manpower, he identified nearly ten potential successors and personally made sure they received good development and testing assignments. He also made sure his board had an opportunity to see each of them in action. As his retirement grew closer, he talked at length with all the potential CEO candidates, with other senior officers, and with the board to see who they felt would be the best successor and why. The discussions focused on the future business environment, on the strengths and weaknesses of the candidates, and on the ''chemistry'' between possible successors and the rest of the management team. During his last eighteen months, Jones narrowed the field to three, and began more actively planning postretirement activities for himself (e.g., board memberships, community and charitable activities). He and his board finally picked Jack Welch, a relatively young executive (forty-four at the time), who was in many ways very different from Jones in background, education, and style, but who clearly fitted the board's image of what would be needed at the top to help the firm excel in the business environments of the late 1980s and 1990s. Then Jones gradually turned over the reins to Welch and left GE (and its board) in an unusually graceful exit.

There are lots of stories about how David Packard kept his line managers focused on practices that facilitate building a leadership capability in management. For example, he did not even allow a corporate personnel department to exist until HP had nearly 1,200 employees. ''The reason for this,'' he has been quoted as saying, ''was that I thought personnel should be everybody's responsibility, and I didn't want to have someone around that they could pass the buck to.''[9]

John Young, the current CEO of HP, is said to be carrying on that tradition in his own way. Because HP's culture is such a central force in producing the kinds of practices described in the last chapter, Young has been known to go out of his way to reinforce core elements of that culture. He is said to do so in dozens of ways. To help support the open and relatively egalitarian norms inherent in that culture, for example, he works in a relatively (by CEO standards) small, open office that has no floor-to-ceiling walls!

At Johnson & Johnson, Chairman James Burke has signaled the importance of leadership by the way he handles promotion discussions. Whenever someone is recommended for promotion to a general management job at Johnson & Johnson, Burke is said always to ask "Who among the next generation of leadership has this person brought into the company or developed?" One can imagine what impact that single question, asked again and again, can have on a firm.

## THE OVERALL PATTERN, POSSIBLE ANTECEDENTS, AND IMPLICATIONS

By now, the primary themes running through this discussion should be clear. That is, the factors that seem to make companies with better managements different from others can be summarized in this way:

1. These firms have more and better programs and practices aimed at finding, developing, retaining, and motivating people with leadership potential.
2. They maintain and enhance those programs and practices, despite short-term business pressures and parochial political pressure, because the line organization works at it. They accept some responsibility for making those programs and practices effective.
3. Line managers work at it because they believe in the importance of those practices to their future prosperity, because the CEO reinforces that belief, and because their corporations' cultures and formal systems provide both appropriate rewards and sanctions.

It is not possible, with the information at hand, to draw any clear conclusions about why one finds that pattern (diagrammed in Exhibit 8–2) much more in some firms than in most. Nevertheless, one can find clues in the history of such corporations; it is

Exhibit 8–2
*What It Takes to Mitigate Short-Term
Economic Pressure and Parochial Politics*

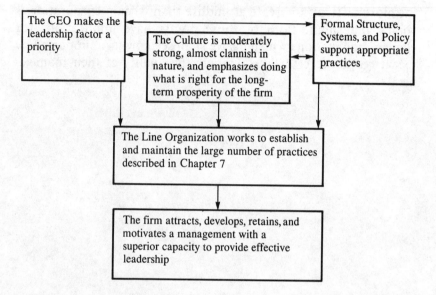

important to recognize those clues explicitly because of their implications for upgrading the quality of one's management (the topic of the next two chapters).

The kinds of firms we have been discussing in this and the previous chapter seem to have a history characterized by one or both of the following: (1) a strong, early CEO, sometimes the firm's founder, who felt leadership was very important and who personally helped develop the patterns shown in Exhibit 8–1, and/ or (2) an industry environment early in the firm's history that was highly competitive and complex and which, in a sense, demanded lots of competent leadership (or put another way, an industry environment that would not tolerate the syndrome summarized in Chapter 5). In other words, firms with superior managements seem to have a history that is different in some critically important ways from corporations like West Products.

If this historical characterization is indeed accurate, it is important to keep two additional points in mind. First of all, this kind of momentum from the past is always subject to decay, especially when people lose sight of how such a pattern helped make them successful in the first place (has that been happening to IBM recently?). Second, the dynamic shown in Exhibit 8–2 is probably far more difficult to create at midlife than when a corporation is young and small. Both of those points have implications for change, implications which (as we shall see now) are supported by recent corporate efforts to upgrade the quality of their managements.

# CHAPTER 9

# Increasing the Quality
# and Quantity of Leadership:
# What Is Being Done Today

W hen asked if there had been any effort in the last five years to try to improve their firms' capacity to attract, develop, and retain the kind of people needed in managerial jobs today, most (73 percent) of the nine hundred executives surveyed by our questionnaire said yes. When asked if those efforts had had any impact, the typical respondent reported that thirty-nine of the forty-six practices listed in the questionnaire had become slightly (usually *very* slightly) more adequate and that none had become less so. That is, the average executive surveyed felt that his or her firm was making some limited (usually very limited) progress on the leadership issue. Around that mean response was a moderately broad range. On the low end, some people felt they were actually sliding backward. On the high end, some felt their firms had made some substantial progress.

As part of the background research for this book, this writer monitored over a three-year period the actions of executives in five corporations who were trying to do something about the issues discussed in this book. Through interviews, a dozen more historical cases were uncovered (although, obviously, in much less depth). In aggregate, those stories tell us a lot about why there is some progress, but why it is so limited. Four of the situations, in particular, are revealing.


## THE "EASTERN FINANCE" STORY

Eastern Finance[1] is a large and well-known firm in the financial services industry. In 1981, the CEO at Eastern decided to upgrade his corporate personnel function by hiring Jack Phillips to be his senior VP for Human Resources. Phillips had spent his entire career, up to that point, at another large firm that had a good reputation for "personnel practices."

Shortly after arriving at Eastern, Phillips concluded in his own mind that the firm was quite unprepared for the growing competition in its industry. In particular, he was concerned about the quality of the firm's management. Among the top twenty-five employees, he could find no obvious candidate to be the next CEO. Among the next two hundred, he could see only three or four people that had the qualities he thought would soon be needed on the Executive Council (the top twenty-five jobs). "Executive resources," Phillips decided, would have to be one of his top priorities.

In January 1982, Phillips created a new job within the corporate HR function, director of Executive Resource Programs, and transferred his most talented HR subordinate into that role. He then charged that person with the task of "developing the very best program possible for upgrading the quality of our senior management." The centerpiece of the program, Phillips decided, would be a succession planning process. Other key components would include a "high-potential identification program," a set of in-house management training programs, and a new computer system which could provide an on-line inventory (backgrounds and "skills") of all managerial personnel at the firm.

Phillips's new director of Executive Resource Programs (ERP) spent the next six months working closely with Phillips and an outside consulting firm. Programs used by Phillips's previous employer were examined in great detail, as were "state-of-the-art" concepts developed by a few university professors, "packaged programs" created by other consulting firms, and the practices employed by one well-known company with a reputation for good management. Eventually, the best that they had found was pulled together and packaged in a thick binder. The first ten pages in the binder explained the overall mission of the new thrust and the goals of the separate component programs. Each program was then explained in detail. The binder also contained copies of all the forms that had to be completed at various times during the year, along with a fairly comprehensive description of how the forms should be filled out.

In mid-August 1982, Phillips spent nearly half a day explaining the new set of programs to his CEO. The boss was interested but skeptical, and asked dozens of questions. Phillips responded to the questioning by selling his program even harder and with more self-confidence. At the conclusion of the meeting, the CEO essentially said: "Listen, Jack, this is your area of expertise, not mine. If you are convinced this is the right thing to do, then we should try it."

The thick binder was reproduced in large numbers, and sent to all middle- and senior-level managers, along with a cover letter from Phillips and a short note from the CEO. At the same time, the ERP director hired three more HR professionals to help him administer the programs.

During the next twelve months (January 1983 to January 1984) the various programs were launched, meetings were held, and forms were completed. All of that activity culminated in a one-day session organized by Phillips but run by the CEO. At that meeting, succession and development plans were reviewed for the top one hundred positions at the firm.

No one was satisfied with the results of the effort after the first year, especially Phillips. But most senior officials, including the CEO, agreed that they had to give the process at least twelve more months. February 1985 was targeted as a date to evaluate the results of the new programs.

By the summer of 1984, well before the evaluation date, evidence began to accumulate that the programs were not working as expected. A review of all senior-level promotions during the first half of 1984 revealed that in nearly half of the cases the person promoted was not the person listed in the succession plans discussed in January. Complaints began to accumulate from the firm's officers to the effect that the new computerized inventory of executive resources was almost useless as a staffing tool (because of both inadequate and inaccurate data). The corporate HR person in charge of the new in-house management development programs found he was unable to get enough candidates nominated by the offices and divisions to fill his classes. Meanwhile, the CEO was encountering more and more negative comments about the programs from his senior managers.

By September of 1984, it was clear to Phillips why those problems existed. Many middle- and senior-level managers were simply not doing what was asked of them. For example, some had turned all responsibility for carrying out the programs over to their personnel staff, people who did not have all the information needed or the authority to make the programs work. Other managers spent minutes on ERP activities instead of the hours that were necessary. In some cases, the managers involved didn't understand what was expected of them. In others, they simply avoided what they felt was an unimportant or a poorly designed activity.

In October 1984, the CEO decided to put the programs on hold until they could be evaluated in February. During the budget discussion in November, all corporate staff departments were asked to reduce headcount by 10 percent, and the CEO suggested to Phillips that he eliminate the four ERP jobs. After a brief struggle to save those jobs, Phillips gave in. In January 1985, someone on the Executive Committee suggested that the February evaluation of ERP was no longer necessary. The majority agreed.

During the rest of 1985, only a few people complained about the loss of the ERP initiative. By the end of the year, most managers seemed to have forgotten about it.

## TYPICAL PROBLEMS

This story about "Eastern" is interesting for our purposes because it appears not to be unusual. Variations of the same story can be found in at least one firm in most industries.[2]

After reading the last five chapters, especially Chapter 8, it should be fairly easy to see the problems inherent in this all too frequent approach. Among other things, the approach is probably:

1. *Not given enough support and involvement from the top.* The CEOs at most firms with superior leadership have provided visible and ongoing support for their approaches to developing managerial excellence.

2. *Too centralized.* Firms that do a better job of attracting, developing, and retaining talent seem to expect and demand that everyone up and down the line help out. They do not try to drive the process from the corporate personnel office.

3. *Too staff-driven.* Firms with strong managerial teams seem to put the primary responsibility for creating those teams on line managers, not on the personnel staff. When IBM first began doing internal management training, for example, it was a district sales manager, not a personnel person, who led the effort.

4. *Unrealistic in terms of what can be accomplished in a short period of time.* Ted Levino, the retired GE executive who helped develop GE's approach to leadership development, has said that it took GE ten years to create its initial set of practices.

5. *Too much of a labor-intensive add-on.* The basic process of attracting, developing, and retaining talent in managerially strong firms seems to be at the very core of each manager's job. It not an unintegrated add-on activity that takes up scarce time from otherwise very busy people.

Both this writer's experiences and data from the Executive Resources Questionnaire (see Table 9–1) suggest that those factors, especially the first two, are particularly common in unsuccessful efforts to improve leadership. In light of the power of the forces that create the syndrome described in Chapter 4, and of the nature

Table 9–1
*Factors That Most Frequently Impede the Success*
*of Efforts to Improve Practices Designed to Strengthen*
*Senior Management Teams: Data from the Questionnaire*

| *Factor* | *How Frequently Does It Impede Efforts?* |
|---|---|
| 1. Lack of top management involvement | 70% of the time |
| 2. New efforts were too centralized | 51% of the time |
| 3. New efforts were too staff-centered | 21% of the time |
| 4. Expectations were unrealistic (too much expected too fast) | 17% of the time |

of the countervailing forces needed to prevent it (described in Chapter 8), those findings should not be surprising.

## THE BRISTOL-MYERS STORY

The Bristol-Myers story is a useful contrast to the "Eastern" story, both in approach and in results to date.[3]

This story begins in the fall of 1983, when the Policy Committee at Bristol-Myers (the top fifteen or so officers) approved with some modifications an initiative from the Corporate Human Resource area to look into the subject of "management development." The initiative, put forth by the senior VP of Human Resources and his Director of Personnel Development, and strongly supported by the CEO, requested that a task force be established, that the task force look into the topic of management development at Bristol-Myers, and that the task force report back to the Policy Committee in about one year.

During the first three months of 1984, Jan Margolis (the corporate director of Personnel Development) led the effort to set up that task force. Its final membership of fourteen people included one person from each of Bristol-Myers's divisions, one person representing corporate staff, an outside expert, and Margolis. The fourteen were carefully selected. They were all people who were well thought of in the corporation. Personnel people were in the minority (three of fourteen). Ages ranged from early thirties to early fifties.

In March, Margolis met individually with all the task force members. She briefed them on their assignment, answered questions, and listened to their initial feelings about management development at Bristol-Myers. The outside expert attended a few of the meetings, and Garth Dimon (her boss) was continually kept informed of progress.

The task force held its first meeting in April 1984 at corporate headquarters on Park Avenue in New York. The morning was spent putting the topic in a broader perspective. The discussion stressed many of the issues identified in the previous chapters of this book, including the difficulty of making much progress on improving the quality of leadership in a short period of time. The afternoon focused on the question, how to proceed? By the end of the day, the group agreed that before the next meeting it needed more information on a number of subjects, including (1) what their various divisions were currently doing in the area of management development, (2) what other companies were doing, and (3) how effective Bristol-Myers's current practices were.

During May, June, and July, considerable information was collected and disseminated to task force members. Two questionnaires were designed and implemented, including the very first version of the Executive Resources Questionnaire. Task force members were encouraged in many ways to initiate an ongoing dialogue with their division presidents and personnel heads on the topic. In addition, at the annual personnel heads meeting in May, a morning was spent specifically dealing with the management development topic.

The task force met again in August for one full day (this time in Chicago). All the information that had been collected was discussed in the morning. In the afternoon, an initial set of recommendations was formulated.

During September and early October, the recommendations were discussed with division and corporate management, including the CEO. In late October, the task force met again to put recommendations in final form. Also in late October, at an off-site three-day meeting of the top forty officers in the company hosted by the CEO, a full morning was devoted to a presentation on the topic.

In December 1984, the task force met with the Policy Committee. Three members of the task force made a formal presentation, giving background on the task force process, on the information it had collected, and on its recommendations. The recommendations, which filled only three single-spaced typed pages, urged that group and division presidents be formally held responsible for finding, developing, and retraining people with potential to provide the corporation with leadership in the future. That primary suggestion, along with secondary support recommendations, was well received.

Late in December, the CEO asked four members of the Policy Committee to look over the recommendations in more depth. They did so during the first six weeks of 1985 and reported back to the Policy Committee that they would support all but one minor idea. At that meeting, the Policy Committee officially endorsed the basic recommendations and asked the original task force for suggestions as to their implementation.

The task force met twice again during April and May. At those meetings, it developed a six-page description of the new management development policy and of guidelines for implementing the policy.

Concurrently, starting in December and ending in June, each of the divisions spent either a half or a full day focusing on basic management development issues. Those sessions, which were funded by corporate headquarters (at the CEO's suggestion) and ultimately involved the top four hundred managers in the company, included a variation of the presentation seen by top management in October. Also during that period, the entire management of the company received a copy of a speech the CEO made to officers in October stressing the importance of "management development." They also received a copy of the 1984 annual report, which contained in a highly visible format an excerpt from that speech.

Starting in July and ending in October 1985, a series of meetings were held with those who would assume primary responsibility for the new process. The meetings were arranged to discuss the specific recommendations, to think through the implications, and to answer any questions. Those involved included group presidents, staff senior vice presidents, division presidents, and, finally, senior personnel heads. At least two task force members plus the Senior HR officer attended each meeting.

Those meetings were the final action taken to set the stage for implementing in the spring of 1986 the key task force recommendation. That recommendation, put succinctly, was that:

- Division presidents and senior corporate staff vice presidents work with their direct reports to identify high-potential employees within their groups, to identify the development needs of those people, and to develop plans for meeting those needs

- Division presidents review the results of that work with their Group VPs at least once a year

- The senior VP of Human Resources communicate the results of those efforts (who all the high potentials are and the plans for their development) to the fifteen top officers of the company

As this was being written, it was currently planned that the original task force would get back together in early 1987 to evaluate how well the corporation had implemented its recommendations (and perhaps to provide additional ideas).

It is too early to tell how successful the effort will be. In terms of concrete results, little has happened so far. Nevertheless, the effort appears to be off to a good start, because, unlike many attempts to improve the quality of a firm's leadership, the approach shows these features:

1. The CEO was very supportive of the effort.
2. Line managers were heavily involved from the beginning.
3. The driving force (the task force) was made up almost entirely of divisional (not corporate) managers.
4. The process was incremental, and from the beginning, expectations for dramatic short-term changes were dampened.

Here we see a case where a CEO, line managers, and HR staff worked together effectively. Unlike the "Eastern Finance" story, this approach at least has a chance of influencing culture, formal systems, and management behavior, and thus having some lasting impact.

## THE CHRYSLER STORY

The approach just described requires time, often lots of time. When firms try to turn a management around quickly, typically because they feel a crisis is imminent, they usually fail. But not always. The Chrysler story is perhaps the best example of a high-risk approach that worked.

The Chrysler management team, before Iacocca arrived, looks significantly different from the team in place three years later. The later team appears both significantly different and much better able to help the firm cope with a competitively intense industry.

The change began, of course, with the arrival of that most unusual man, Lee Iacocca. Even his first day on the job, Iacocca had most of the attributes listed in Exhibit 3-1 ("Some of the Personal Requirements for Effective Leadership"). He lacked only internal knowledge about Chrysler and some of the inside relationships he would need to lead. To help make up for that deficiency, he immediately chose, as a second in command, a well-regarded Chrysler executive whom he had once known and re-spected at Ford. That man provided Iacocca with the eyes and ears that he had yet to develop inside the firm.

Iacocca's second step in putting together a new management team was to persuade a number of Ford executives, including some who had recently retired, to come to work for him at Chrysler. They were people he knew and respected, people who already knew how to work together, and people whom Iacocca (and proba-bly Iacocca alone) was able to attract to what many considered a sinking ship.

Step three focused internally. An aggressive search was made for young people with leadership potential, as well as for oldtimers who had been overlooked (or ignored) by the previous regime. Hundreds of people were brought into new jobs through this process—a process driven by Iacocca and his new team of top executives.

Step four focused on creating some of the conditions that would encourage, allow, and help those people to provide leadership. This step had numerous components. Iacocca empowered his man-agers with his new vision and strategies (which in turn made it much easier for them to develop their own agendas). He also began to cut out bureaucracy and levels and staff, thus making it easier actually to lead, and at the same time making it more difficult to play the old bureaucratic games.

All those steps took about three years (which, in the world of large corporations, is movement at the speed of light). And they were unusually effective. Credit goes mostly to Iacocca, both for what he brought to the situation and for not making the error that one commonly sees in situations like this: bringing in far too many outsiders from far too many different corporate cultures.

In a sense, step five is still being carried out today, nearly a decade after Iacocca joined Chrysler. Step five represents an at-tempt to establish the culture and practices that can create a management strong enough to lead the firm when Iacocca retires. At this point, it is not clear how well the final step is progressing.

## THE EDWARD ROBBINS STORY

Neither the "Eastern Finance," nor the Bristol-Myers story, and certainly not the Chrysler story, represents the norm today. Most systematic corporatewide efforts to upgrade leadership capability fall somewhere between "Eastern Finance" and Bristol-Myers. Most crisis-driven situations are much less successful than the Chrysler story. More typical than any of those situations are stories that are less visible and dramatic. In a sense, they represent isolated attempts by sometimes courageous individuals to make a difference.

Edward Robbins[4] is typical of this group. He is in his mid-forties and is in charge of an organization with approximately 5,000 employees, inside a manufacturing firm that has a world-wide employment of 50,000. Edward is convinced for both business and personal reasons that developing a stronger leadership capacity in his organization is vitally important. Ever since his promotion into his current job, he has been pursuing that goal aggressively and successfully, despite little encouragement from his bosses.

Unlike most of his peers, Edward approaches organizational development the same way he approaches market development and product development—it becomes a part of his daily dialogue with his managers. Just as he looks for opportunities each and every day to make some progress on his marketing and product agenda, he also seeks opportunities to work on his management development agenda. Often that manifests itself in questions. At the end of a market forecast meeting, when young George's name comes up in the conversation, Edward asks if George is developing the type of customer relationships that he will eventually need to provide leadership in bigger and bigger sales management jobs. When Edward sees a manager who he knows had recently been recruiting at a major university, he asks how the recruiting effort is going. When he travels to a branch office in another city, he takes a few minutes to meet a young woman who has recently been identified by the branch manager as having high potential.

Edward also spends a day with his direct reports, at least once a year, reviewing who they think have potential, what those people's development needs are, and plans for meeting those needs. Although he receives little help from the rest of the company in meeting the development needs of his people, he aggressively looks for ways to meet those needs in his own organization and pressures his managers to do so too.

The company's personnel function does virtually nothing to support Edward's development efforts. But Edward has taught his own personnel assistant how to help. And help he does, with enthusiasm.

If you talk to people in Edward's organization, they will quickly point out that he is a very good role model. Most say that they have learned something about leadership within a managerial context by watching him. They will stress that he gives them opportunities to provide leadership. Edward doesn't smother them with bureaucracy or micromanagement from above. He takes some risks, and they very much appreciate that fact.

Because most of the rest of the firm does little to find and develop managerial talent, Edward's group stands out and is occasionally raided to staff jobs elsewhere. That obviously makes life in the short term more difficult for Edward, but it appears to help him in the moderate to long term in two ways. First of all, with more than a few of "Edward's people" in key jobs outside his group, he is able to get an unusual degree of cooperation and assistance from outside his part of the organization, which helps his group perform better than it could by itself. Second, with a growing number of respected people throughout the company thinking very well of Edward, he has as good a chance as anyone at becoming the firm's next CEO.

Edward's efforts are obviously not turning his firm into a managerial powerhouse, but they are making a difference.

## THE OVERALL STATE OF THE LEADERSHIP ISSUE: AN ASSESSMENT

While conducting background research for this book, this writer encountered hundreds of managers in dozens of corporations who were thinking about some of the issues dealt with in previous chapters. In many cases, only preliminary discussions were involved. In other cases, one finds efforts of the sort seen in the Robbins, Bristol-Myers, Chrysler, and Eastern Finance stories. Overall, one gets the sense (supported by the questionnaire data) that some progress is being made, but it is clearly limited progress.

There are probably many reasons why more firms are not adapting more swiftly and successfully to the changes discussed in Chapter 1. Part of the problem in some cases is simply a lack of awareness of those changes, or the implications that follow. One gets the sense that most people these days see the change in competitive intensity but don't entirely appreciate what that implies for managerial jobs (the leadership issue). But an even bigger part probably relates to the difficulty of change. Overcoming the short-term economic and the parochial political forces is tough. Creating a culture that can continuously buffer an organization against those forces may be even tougher. Even maintaining a good culture, once established, seems to be a real challenge (indeed, in some of the firms described in Chapter 7, growth, diversification, and short-term economic pressures seem to be eroding the cultures that have served them so well in the past).

There appear to be no easy answers here. Nevertheless, implicit in the analysis presented throughout the book are some additional thoughts that should be helpful. We shall focus on those explicitly in the final chapter.

# CHAPTER 10

# Increasing the Quality and Quantity of Leadership:
## What Else Is Needed

Despite the efforts documented in Chapter 9, a significant number of firms are still a long way from having the leadership capacity they need to excel today. Though many may be moving in the right direction, progress seems to be coming very slowly. In some cases, firms are clearly making no progress at all.

In this final chapter, I am going to outline what I personally believe is needed if we are to achieve significant additional progress on these issues. As you will see, I don't think there are any simple answers. Even the cleverest of gimmicks and techniques are not powerful enough to change corporate cultures, and that is surely what is needed in many cases. Something more fundamental is necessary.

Just as vision helps leaders to produce change that eludes managers and bureaucrats, powerful ideas can transform situations that are impervious to programs, tools, or simplistic advice. New ideas are what we need—or, more precisely, new ways of thinking about some very basic issues.

122

## THINKING ABOUT MANAGERIAL JOBS

It would help greatly if we could take the concept of the professional manager who can manage anything and drive a stake through its ever so resilient heart. That concept is still very influential today, despite some people's efforts to demonstrate the problems with it. It haunts MBA education. It influences how managers think about their careers (sometimes in most destructive ways). It is used to justify tragic staffing decisions, some of the more outrageous acquisitions by raiders, and many of the least successful diversification efforts seen in the last two decades.

The problem with the concept is not in the pioneering thinking that led to its birth. Like all "professions," management needs some ethical standards. And it is generic: basic tools for market research, accounting, inventory control, and competitive analysis can be applied (more or less) anywhere. The problem with the concept is that managerial jobs today require more than management. Most important, as we have seen here, they require leadership. Good planning, budgeting, organizing, and controlling are no longer sufficient. One also needs good visions, strategies, coalitions, and motivation to deal with competitively intense business environments.

Unlike management, the requirements for leadership include some things that are very situation-specific and that tend to take time, often much time, to develop. This is why no one has ever dreamed of suggesting the concept of the "professional leader." Of course, all this does not preclude the existence of a few unusually broad and talented people who can move easily across industries and companies. There will always be some people like that. But they will always be rare. And even those people will have limits to what they can manage.

For the foreseeable future at least, most managerial jobs will have a leadership component to them. Big jobs will usually require a lot of leadership. It is time we explicitly recognize that in the way we think about those jobs. When we do, it will have a powerful impact on how we staff managerial jobs and on how we go about developing people for those jobs. It will also shape (for the better) how we think about business strategies, especially regarding acquisitions.

## THINKING ABOUT LEADERSHIP

Mention the word "leadership," and the vast majority of folks will think of Gandhi or Churchill or Iacocca. In doing so, they raise the concept to a level where it seems relevant to a handful of people at most. Thinking that way, the young manager doesn't try to develop her own leadership potential, because, after all, she realizes that she is just a mortal and was surely not *born* a *leader*. Thinking that same way, her boss does nothing to develop that potential either (after all, the boss rationalizes, the kid is not a young Iacocca). The same boss also does not worry about "leadership" when recruiting (finding the next Leader, he points out, is surely the CEO's job). The overall effect of all those actions is obviously enormous.

Leadership, with a small "l," is of incredible importance in today's world. Its cumulative effect often makes the difference between dreadfully stifling and unresponsive bureaucracies and lively, adaptive organizations. At the level of a single individual, it sometimes occurs in such a subtle way that we don't even notice it. That is especially true if the vision is "borrowed" (developed not by the individual but by someone else) and the number of people who must be led is very small, as is so often the case.

Needless to say, it would help greatly if we could get more people to think of leadership in the small "l" sense, and not just in the larger-than-life capital "L" sense. That would force a re-evaluation of the current practices shaping the careers of large numbers of people inside firms. It would also force managers to consider leadership potential in virtually all hiring decisions (which, in turn, would probably have the additional benefit of forcing more firms to broaden their labor markets by more aggressively pursuing women, minorities, and foreigners).

## THINKING ABOUT MANAGERIAL CAREERS

To a large degree today, managerial careers are thought of as beginning with an educational program and then proceeding through a series of promotions and salary increases into bigger and bigger jobs. Those careers are not thought of as a continuing developmental process in which people become equipped (with business knowledge, track records, good working relationships, additional skills) to handle more and more difficult challenges, especially leadership challenges. As a result, some very talented people manage their careers today in self-destructive ways. Among other things, they get themselves into trouble by paying far too much attention to salary increases and promotions and far too little attention to their own development needs and ways of meeting those needs.

Gerald Stanton (Chapter 4) is in many ways typical. If, for example, he had been managing his own career competently for long-term gain, he might have found a way to get a lateral move out of the retail division, for developmental purposes, long before the incident that sent his career crashing into a stone wall. Such a move would have slowed down his vertical movement and his salary increases, but if done well, it could have (1) exposed him to a broader part of the business; (2) extended his contact base beyond just retailing; (3) provided him with role models and teachers who were a lot more useful than the retail head, Joe Clark; and (4) put him in an environment where the jobs were more doable and where it was more likely that he could continue to build a strong track record.

Competent career management can be thought of as having three components: self-assessment, opportunity assessment, and proactive career planning.[1] The first involves periodically thinking through issues associated with career objectives, with one's own developmental progress, and with remaining development needs. The second involves looking for feasible options for meeting those development needs. The third component takes those insights and creates plans based on them (see Exhibit 10-1).

If more people thought about their careers in the manner shown in Exhibit 10-1, it would have a most powerful impact on leadership development. Decisions about how to use job experiences to develop Harry or Harriett would be made with much greater sophistication (and thus would be more efficient and effective).

As an educator, I am painfully aware that our educational system does not do a good job of teaching young people to think about their careers in that way. This, too, needs to change.

Exhibit 10–1
*Competent Career Management*

A. *Self-assessment*

1.  What are my career objectives?

2.  How am I doing on dimensions relevant to those objectives?
    • Business knowledge
    • Organizational knowledge
    • Good working relationships
    • Relationships to mentors
    • Interpersonal skills
    • Intellectual skills
    • Track record of accomplishments
    • Reputation

3.  In light of the above, what are my biggest developmental needs?

B. *Opportunity Assessment*

1.  What job or job sequence options are feasible in the near future for me?

2.  In terms of each option:
    • How well does it fit career objectives?
    • How well does it fit developmental needs?
    • Do I have what it takes to perform well?

3.  What other possibilities might be available and how can each help meet developmental needs?
    • Special projects/assignments?
    • Training programs?

C. *Proactive Career Planning*

1.  In light of the self and opportunity assessments, what career plans for the next 1-5 years make sense, taking into account short-term business realities and political realities?

2.  How can I sell those plans upward to key bosses and mentors so as to get agreement and commitment?

## THINKING ABOUT THE ROLE OF HUMAN RESOURCE PROFESSIONALS

When commitment from the top to building a strong management team is lacking, and when the line organization follows the lead from the CEO and basically ignores the issue, HR people are sometimes tempted to grab leadership as their issue and to try to make it happen by themselves. They develop management training courses (despite the fact that no top people are asking for such courses). They develop a succession planning process, and try to force line managers to engage in it. They go to college campuses and try to recruit high potentials. They create special programs for "their" high-potential recruits. They, they, they.

The attitude behind that approach is something like this: (1) Attracting and developing a management that can supply effective leadership is important to the future of the company, but (2) it doesn't get any support from the line, so since (3) we know something about that (it is a human resource activity!), (4) we have a responsibility to make it happen by doing it ourselves.

That approach seems never to work. As a matter of fact, it sometimes produces more harm than doing nothing at all. Yet smart, capable, caring people get seduced into that approach all the time.

The underlying problem here, somewhat ironically, relates back to leadership. Colleges and most corporations teach HR professionals (and almost every one else) to be technically competent individual contributors. They teach them how to do things by themselves. They do precious little to help people learn how to get things done through others when one has little or no formal control of those others. They do not show them how to be leaders. And yet that is precisely what staff HR professionals need, especially when commitment is lacking from the top to HR issues.

Most of my last book, *Power and Influence: Beyond Formal Authority*, spoke to this aspect of the leadership issue, and I'm not going to try to rehash all that. The key points of relevance here in summary are:

1. HR people have got to stop conceptualizing their role as a "professional" individual contributor and realize that their job is to help provide corporations with leadership on HR issues.
2. Providing leadership means influencing other managers to take responsibility for finding, developing, retaining, and motivating talent, and influencing them to approach that responsibility in a sensible way (as outlined earlier in this book).

3. Successful influence of that sort cannot be based on wielding formal authority. It is no use trying to order or to force managers. Successful influence must be based on other sources of power: relevant information, good working relationships, reputation, interpersonal and intellectual skills, track record, and so on.
4. Developing those sources of power, which do not automatically come with an HR job, has to receive a much higher priority than it has today among many human resource professionals.

The message inherent in those four deceptively simple points is, unfortunately, not a message some HR people want to hear. Yet until they come to grips with those issues, they will continue to play a marginal role, especially in firms where commitment to key HR issues is missing in upper management, firms where their assistance is most needed.

## THINKING ABOUT MANAGING GLOBAL BUSINESSES

Many if not most corporations are becoming players in global industries.[2] Ongoing advances in communications and transportation will probably help continue that trend, at least in the foreseeable future.

Some businesses are beginning to think about themselves as "global players." Yet few businesses seem to be thinking seriously about the managerial implications involved.

A truly global business probably needs a truly global management—a management that understands and is comfortable in a broad range of nations and cultures. But today, no major U.S. corporation has a highly internationalized management, no matter how one defines internationalized.[3] Some well-known firms have senior management teams with virtually no non-U.S. experience. This writer has visited corporations that do business in more than fifty countries outside the United States but who have no one in their top twenty to thirty positions who has ever spent more than two years outside the United States. Some well-known firms have even used their international operations as a dumping ground for managers who have failed.

Creating an internationalized management is not easy. For an

American corporation, it can be difficult to attract and integrate non-Americans into what is clearly an American firm. Persuading talented young U.S. employees to accept an assignment overseas can be even tougher, especially in light of dual career problems and the often short-term career focus one finds these days. Getting people repatriated, once they have gone abroad, is also a challenge; for some, the move back to the United States can be even more difficult than the move abroad (especially if their original mentors and supporters have "forgotten" them).

Nevertheless, there is evidence that those problems can (at least partially) be overcome. Nearly half of the top fifty officers at Coca Cola were born abroad, and all of the top technical people are reported to have had at least a three-year assignment outside their home countries. By 1990, a third of the top thirty-five executives at Johnson & Johnson are expected to have considerable international experience (through career assignments or foreign birth). Today, about half of the top eighty-six people at Morgan Guaranty have spent two or more years outside the United States.

More firms need to be thinking about all this.

## THINKING ABOUT SOURCES
## OF COMPETITIVE ADVANTAGE

Consider for a moment the kinds of factors that served as key sources of competitive advantage for many firms in the 1950s and 1960s. Five of the most prominent factors back then were:

1. *A large market share in a growing market.* Winners in the 1950s and 1960s tended to dominate markets more than the also-rans, and they tended to dominate the faster-growing market niches. The dominance gave them the economies of scale associated with superior profits, which allowed them to invest more in whatever it took to defend their market position (e.g., new product development, advertising).

2. *Patents for products that had a growing demand.* In some industries, patents essentially gave the winners back then a monopoly on some of the best products, and that monopoly provided them with their superior economic performance. The winners then used some of that profitability to surround

key patents with layer after layer of additional patents, extending their advantage over time.

3. *Large capacity in highly capital-intensive industries with growing markets.* With demand booming after World War II, companies in some highly capital-intensive industries with the capacity to handle product demand made great profits, which allowed them to add more capacity and to add it faster than the also-rans (who simply did not have the needed financing). And the high capital requirements provided a barrier to entry that kept out new potential competitors (especially non-U.S. competition, which was either always poor or financially ruined by World War II).

4. *Favorable government regulation.* Winners in some industries were able to stay on top because legislation and government policies essentially kept out new competitors and gave them the upper hand over existing competition. The winners then invested some of their superior profits in lobbying efforts to maintain or increase the legislation that favored them.

5. *Control of key sources of supply.* In some industries, a key reason why the winners won was that they had greater control over the key raw materials needed to compete in their industry. In other words, if you owned most of the places where top-quality bananas grew, and the demand for bananas was good, your banana business did very well.

There are, of course, still other factors that were important sources of competitive advantage in the 1950s and 1960s. But those five are certainly representative of the most important ones.

The reason the list is so interesting, and the reason it is so important to recognize explicitly such "winning" traits from the recent past, is that *THE WORLD IS CHANGING* in ways that will probably make those factors less powerful in the future. Business strategies based on a correct analysis of what worked yesterday could be a recipe for disaster today.

Most futurologists agree on three fundamental points about what is changing. Contrasting today and the foreseeable future to the decades immediately after World War II, they see in most industries

1. More competition

2. More international competition
3. More well-financed international competition

Immediately after World War II, much of the developed world lay in shambles. It was either bombed out or broke or both. Developing countries had little money or industry. Transportation and communication infrastructures were puny, at least compared with today. In that world, competition in most industries was *relatively* moderate, domestic or regional in scope (except for some U.S. exporters), and among firms that rarely had big bank accounts.

In the past forty years, that has changed radically, and it is continuing to change. Today we find well-financed German, U.S., and Korean firms fighting it out in some industries, while big Japanese, Brazilian, and British firms attack each other in other industries.

Those changes have enormously important implications. In a world of aggressive and well-financed competition, the most common factors that helped many firms to excel a few decades ago are often no longer *protectable* sources of competitive advantage. This is not to say that those factors are irrelevant today. Some will continue to be important, especially in certain industries. But on the average, they will be less important for some perfectly predictable reasons.

Consider the earlier list of five factors. First there was "a large market share in a growing market." Without question, that is still important today. But if the Japanese have taught us anything in the past two decades, it is that market share can be bought out from under you by a well-financed and patient competitor. He just enters your market with a reasonable product, prices it low, and accepts low or no return while he gains market share.

Patents (item 2) are also still important, but often less so, especially in the ever-expanding service sector of the economy. But even in manufacturing, patents are most effective when technology is developing slowly. When technological development speeds up faster and faster, patents become less and less effective competitive tools. Today, the speed of technological development is increasing because of, among other things, the emergence of more and more competitors who are wealthy enough to put a lot of money into R&D. And if R&D does not pay off, a rich firm can often buy the company that has the patent, or else lease the rights.[4]

The third historical source of competitive advantage was capacity in a capital-intensive industry. It too is still a potential source of competitive advantage, but again, less so. Look at steel. The biggest U.S. steel companies did very well just after World War II. But now the Japanese and others have the money to build new plants using more modern technology. Those plants tend to be much more efficient than the old U.S. plants. But U.S. competitors find that writing off the old plants and building new ones is incredibly difficult. So the Japanese (and Brazilians and Koreans) win out, while what used to be a great asset is now an albatross around the neck of some U.S. corporations.

The relevance today of government regulation (factor 4) should be easy to see. In many industries we are getting, and we will continue to get, less and less regulation, as aggressive competitors use their money to lobby in Washington and state capitals for "freer" trade and a more "competitive" system (always wearing white hats and pleading the case of the consumer). We have already seen it in the airline, trucking, telephone, and banking industries. There is undoubtedly still more to come.

That leaves one last item on the list: controlling sources of key raw materials. Again, it is fairly easy to see that this factor doesn't go very far in protecting a firm today. Rich competitors can afford to invest money looking for new sources of those materials or, if necessary, to buy them (islands, oil fields, gold mines) at a premium price.

In other words, a number of the most fundamental sources of competitive advantage that helped many firms excel during the recent past will be less helpful in the future, basically because those factors can be easily purchased (e.g., capacity or patents) or destroyed (e.g., regulation) by aggressive and rich competitors. And the number of aggressive and rich competitors seems to continue to grow yearly.

All that raises an obvious question. What factor, if any, that can provide a competitive advantage, is sustainable over time because a fat checkbook cannot necessarily buy it or take it away? The cynical side of most people will quickly answer that anything can be arranged with a big checkbook. But that is surely not true. There are a few things that money may not be able to buy the financially well-off also-ran, one of which is the topic of this book.

*A firm that has taken the time to develop practices and programs that build strong management teams able to provide a business with effective leadership has a most powerful source of competitive advantage today.* And even if a firm is competing against a very rich and very large corporation, if that competitor does not have comparable practices, it may well require a decade to develop the conditions that can sustain those practices.[5] And during the ten-year period, the firm with strong leadership has a chance, in a truly competitive environment, to pulverize the competition.

This analysis brings us back to the question of how to think about the issues raised in this book. The problem today is that many people consider these issues either esoteric (e.g., leadership is about Gandhi and Churchill) or "personnel" trivialities (e.g., recruiting), or possibly both. That is, they fail to see that the business environment today has, in a sense, democratized leadership, making it relevant not for the few but for the many. They also fail to recognize (or refuse to acknowledge) that whether the many are prepared for the leadership challenge is directly a function of core organizational practices, not peripheral "personnel programs." And in the broadest sense, they fail to realize that what we are discussing here is how a changing business environment is shifting the bases of competitive advantage, and thus of what will be required to excel in the future.

This must change.

# APPENDIX

# The Executive Resources Questionnaire

DIRECTIONS: Please give your <u>candid</u> evaluation of how good a job your Corporation is doing with respect to issues associated with its executive resources.

PART I

Recruiting and Hiring

1. How good a job is the company doing with respect to recruiting and hiring a sufficient number of people into the firm who have the potential of someday providing effective leadership in important management positions? (Circle one)

   Excellent  /  Very Good  /  Good  /  Fair  /  Poor

2. What about 5 years ago? How good a job was the company then doing with respect to recruiting and hiring a sufficient number of people who had the potential of someday providing effective leadership in important management positions? (Circle one)

   Excellent  /  Very Good  /  Good  /  Fair  /  Poor

DIRECTIONS: Below is a list of programs and practices which affect the type and the quality of people brought into the firm. First, please rate <u>how well each today supports</u> the objective of attracting a sufficient number of people who have the potential of someday providing effective leadership in important management positions (<u>circle</u> the appropriate number). Next think about the situation 5 years ago, and consider if you would have answered the same question differently. If yes, put a <u>check</u> by the number that best describes the situation back then. If the situation has not changed, circle the "no change" option. PLEASE REREAD THESE DIRECTIONS TO MAKE SURE YOU UNDERSTAND THEM.

- 2 -

| | More than Adequately Supports the Objective | Adequately Supports the Need | Somewhat Adequately Supports the Need | Inadequately Supports the Need | Was this different 5 years ago? (If no, circle no. If yes put a ✓ by the number on the left that best describes the situation back then.) |
|---|---|---|---|---|---|
| 3. The strategic/business and human resource planning processes which help clarify what kind of a company will exist in 5-10 years, and thus how many and what kind of important management positions will need to be staffed then. | 1 | 2 | 3 | 4 | No Change |
| 4. The firm's college recruiting efforts | 1 | 2 | 3 | 4 | No Change |
| 5. The standards used by hiring-managers in recruiting people | 1 | 2 | 3 | 4 | No Change |
| 6. The capacity of hiring-managers to identify and select high-potential people | 1 | 2 | 3 | 4 | No Change |
| 7. The firm's starting salaries | 1 | 2 | 3 | 4 | No Change |
| 8. The kind of entry level positions offered to people | 1 | 2 | 3 | 4 | No Change |
| 9. Special programs offered to high-potential hires | 1 | 2 | 3 | 4 | No Change |
| 10. The benefits available to new employees | 1 | 2 | 3 | 4 | No Change |

- 3 -

| | | More than Adequately Supports the Objective | Adequately Supports the Need | Somewhat Adequately Supports the Need | Inadequately Supports the Need | Was this different 5 years ago? (If no, circle no. If yes put a ✓ by the number on the left that best describes the situation back then.) |
|---|---|---|---|---|---|---|
| 11. | The training/educational opportunities available to new employees | 1 | 2 | 3 | 4 | No Change |
| 12. | The company's reputation as an affirmative action employer | 1 | 2 | 3 | 4 | No Change |
| 13. | The promotional opportunities available to employees | 1 | 2 | 3 | 4 | No Change |
| 14. | The firm's compensation structure and practices | 1 | 2 | 3 | 4 | No Change |
| 15. | The company's culture and work environment | 1 | 2 | 3 | 4 | No Change |
| 16. | The company's reputation | 1 | 2 | 3 | 4 | No Change |
| 17. | The amount of carefully planned time and effort the company expends trying to manage the whole process of recruiting and hiring people with high potential | 1 | 2 | 3 | 4 | No Change |

PART II

Training and Development

18. How good a job is the company doing with respect to developing high-potential employees? (Circle one)

    Excellent  /  Very good  /  Good  /  Fair  /  Poor

- 4 -

19.  Five years ago, how good a job was the company doing with respect to developing high-potential employees?  (Circle one)

Excellent  /  Very good  /  Good  /  Fair  /  Poor

DIRECTIONS:  Below is a list of programs and practices which affect how good a job the company is doing with respect to spotting high-potential people, identifying their developmental needs, and then meeting those needs.  As you just did in Part II, please first rate how well each of these items contribute today to the objective of developing sufficient executives for the future (circle the appropriate number).  Then consider 5 years ago, and put a √ by the appropriate number if the situation was different then.  (If it has not changed, again circle "no change.")

| | | More than Adequately Supports the Objective | Adequately Supports the Need | Somewhat Adequately Supports the Need | Inadequately Supports the Need | Was this different 5 years ago?  (If no, circle no.  If yes, put a √ by the number on the left that best describes the situation back then.) |
|---|---|---|---|---|---|---|
| 20. | The regular performance appraisal process | 1 | 2 | 3 | 4 | No Change |
| 21. | Special programs for spotting high-potential employees | 1 | 2 | 3 | 4 | No Change |
| 22. | The opportunities offered to people to get them exposure to higher levels of management | 1 | 2 | 3 | 4 | No Change |
| 23. | Formal succession planning reviews | 1 | 2 | 3 | 4 | No Change |
| 24. | The capacity of the firm's executives to identify people with potential | 1 | 2 | 3 | 4 | No Change |

- 5 -

| | | More than Adequately Supports the Objective | Adequately Supports the Need | Somewhat Adequately Supports the Need | Inadequately Supports the Need | Was this different 5 years ago? (If no, circle no. If yes put a ✓ by the number on the left that best describes the situation back then.) |
|---|---|---|---|---|---|---|
| 25. | The capacity of the firm's managers to identify the developmental needs of high-potential people | 1 | 2 | 3 | 4 | No Change |
| 26. | Special programs aimed at identifying the developmental needs of high-potential people | 1 | 2 | 3 | 4 | No Change |
| 27. | The way special jobs are used to develop high-potential people | 1 | 2 | 3 | 4 | No Change |
| 28. | The way responsibilities are added to the current jobs of high-potential people for development purposes | 1 | 2 | 3 | 4 | No Change |
| 29. | The firm's use of in-company management training programs | 1 | 2 | 3 | 4 | No Change |
| 30. | The firm's participation in outside management training programs | 1 | 2 | 3 | 4 | No Change |
| 31. | The number and type of lateral transfers made for developmental purposes inside divisions | 1 | 2 | 3 | 4 | No Change |

| | More than Adequately Supports the Objective | Adequately Supports the Need | Somewhat Adequately Supports the Need | Inadequately Supports the Need | Was this different 5 years ago? (If no, circle no. If yes put a √ by the number on the left that best describes the situa- tion back then.) |
|---|---|---|---|---|---|
| 32. The number and type of lateral transfers made for developmental purposes across divisions | 1 | 2 | 3 | 4 | No Change |
| 33. The mentoring, role modeling, and coaching provided | 1 | 2 | 3 | 4 | No Change |
| 34. The instruction given to high-potentials regarding how to manage their own careers for long-term development | 1 | 2 | 3 | 4 | No Change |
| 35. The way managers are rewarded for developing subordinates | 1 | 2 | 3 | 4 | No Change |
| 36. The way developmental needs are discussed with subordinates and joint plans are made about what and how to improve | 1 | 2 | 3 | 4 | No Change |
| 37. The way feedback is given to subordinates regarding developmental progress | 1 | 2 | 3 | 4 | No Change |
| 38. The amount of carefully planned time and effort the company expends trying to manage the whole process of developing high-potential people | 1 | 2 | 3 | 4 | No Change |

- 7 -

PART III

### Retention and Motivation

39. How good a job is the company doing with respect to retaining and motivating high-potential employees? (Circle one)

   Excellent  /  Very Good  /  Good  /  Fair  /  Poor

40. Five years ago, how good a job did the company do with respect to retaining and motivating high-potential employees? (Circle one)

   Excellent  /  Very Good  /  Good  /  Fair  /  Poor

DIRECTIONS:  Below is a list of programs and practices which affect how well the company is doing with respect to retaining and motivating high-potential employees. Please rate how well each does this today (with a circle). Then, if the situation was different 5 years ago, use a √ to rate how the item supported the objective back then.

| | More than Adequately Supports the Objective | Adequately Supports the Need | Somewhat Adequately Supports the Need | Inadequately Supports the Need | Was this different 5 years ago? (If no, circle no. If yes, put a √ by the number on the left that best describes the situation back then.) |
|---|---|---|---|---|---|
| 41. The firm's compensation practices | 1 | 2 | 3 | 4 | No Change |
| 42. The promotion opportunities offered to high-potentials | 1 | 2 | 3 | 4 | No Change |
| 43. The developmental job opportunities available | 1 | 2 | 3 | 4 | No Change |
| 44. In-house training opportunities | 1 | 2 | 3 | 4 | No Change |
| 45. Outside training opportunities | 1 | 2 | 3 | 4 | No Change |
| 46. The information available to high-potentials on job openings in the company | 1 | 2 | 3 | 4 | No Change |

- 8 -

| | More than Adequately Supports the Objective | Adequately Supports the Need | Somewhat Adequately Supports the Need | Inadequately Supports the Need | Was this different 5 years ago? (If no, circle no. If yes put a ✓ by the number on the left that best describes the situation back then.) |
|---|---|---|---|---|---|
| 47. The quality of career planning discussions with their bosses | 1 | 2 | 3 | 4 | No Change |
| 48. The firm's incentive compensation plans | 1 | 2 | 3 | 4 | No Change |
| 49. The firm's benefit package | 1 | 2 | 3 | 4 | No Change |
| 50. The company's fundamental concern and caring for its employees | 1 | 2 | 3 | 4 | No Change |
| 51. The company's culture and work environment | 1 | 2 | 3 | 4 | No Change |
| 52. The amount of carefully planned time and effort the company expends trying to manage the whole process of retaining and motivating high-potential people | 1 | 2 | 3 | 4 | No Change |

## PART IV

### Improvement Efforts

53. During the recent past (the past 5 or so years), has the company, or some group in the company, tried to improve your capacity to attract, develop, and retain high-potential people?

Yes _____      No _____

- 9 -

54. If yes, how successful have they been?

    Very Successful   /   Somewhat Successful   /   Not Successful

55. Which, if any, of the following factors contributed to the success of this effort? (Check as many as applicable)

    \_\_\_\_ Top management support

    \_\_\_\_ Top management involvement

    \_\_\_\_ The addition of new human resource staff positions

    \_\_\_\_ Other (Specify) _____

    _____

    _____

56. Which, if any, of the following factors impeded the success of this effort? (Check no more than three.)

    \_\_\_\_ New efforts were too staff centered

    \_\_\_\_ New efforts were too centralized

    \_\_\_\_ New efforts were too decentralized

    \_\_\_\_ New programs took up too much management time

    \_\_\_\_ Lack of top management support

    \_\_\_\_ Lack of top management involvement

    \_\_\_\_ Expectations were unrealistic (too much expected too quickly)

    \_\_\_\_ Not enough staff resources available

    \_\_\_\_ Other (Specify) _____

    _____

    _____

- 10 -

## PART V

### An Overall Evaluation

57. In 5-10 years, if nothing changes, what percentage of the important management positions in the company will be staffed by people who are ideally suited for their positions? (Circle one)

My estimate is - Under 10%    40 - 49%    70 - 79%
                 10 - 19%      50 - 59%    80 - 89%
                 20 - 29%      60 - 69%    Over 90%
                 30 - 39%

58. For reference purposes, what percentage of the important management positions in the company are currently staffed by people who are ideally suited for their positions? (Circle one)

My estimate is - Under 10%    40 - 49%    70 - 79%
                 10 - 19%      50 - 59%    80 - 89%
                 20 - 29%      60 - 69%    Over 90%
                 30 - 39%

59. Five years ago, what percentage of the important management positions were then staffed with people ideally suited for those positions? (Circle one)

My estimate is - Under 10%    40 - 49%    70 - 79%
                 10 - 19%      50 - 59%    80 - 89%
                 20 - 29%      60 - 69%    Over 90%
                 30 - 39%

# Notes

Preface (*pp. vii–ix*)

1. A summary description of much of this work can be found in my last book, *Power and Influence: Beyond Formal Authority*. See Kotter (1985), pp. 193–98.

Chapter 1 (*pp. 5–15*)

1. When asked "Is the competitive intensity in your industry about the same today, or greater, or less than in the 1950s and 1960s?," more than 90 percent of the executives interviewed as background for this book responded (without hesitation) "greater." In many cases the response was "much greater." For other evidence of this trend, see Bower (1985), and Scott and Lodge (1985).
2. Ford, Chrysler, Toyota, Nissan, Honda, Volkswagen/Audi, Volvo, Daimler-Benz, Saab, Renault, and Mazda.
3. There are still other changes contributing to the surge in competitive intensity (e.g., technological change), but these are probably the most important ones.
4. See, for example, "Rebuilding to Survive," *Time*, February 16, 1987, pp. 44–45.
5. Before deregulation (1978), there were thirty-five domestic airlines. The number jumped to nearly one hundred by 1981, according to the FAA.
6. Internal GE documents.
7. U.S. Health Care Financing Administration, *Health Care Financing Review*, Fall 1985 and earlier issues.
8. As reported in *Time* magazine, July 28, 1986, pp. 29 and 33.
9. *GM Today* 12, no. 5 (June 19, 1986): 1.
10. See, for example, Lieberson and O'Connor (1972), Carroll (1984), Gamson and Scotch (1964), Grusky (1963), Salancik and Pfeffer (1972).

## Chapter 2 (*pp. 16–27*)

1. Measuring "effective leadership" with any degree of precision is enormously difficult, for a number of reasons. See note 7 below.

2. Iacocca and Novak (1984) and interviews with Chrysler executives.

3. Reported in Kotter and Lawrence (1974).

4. Reported in Kotter (1982).

5. See Bennis and Nanus (1985), Levinson and Rosenthal (1984), and McCall and Lombardo (1983). Interesting work by Bass (1985) and Tichy and Devanna (1986) is also basically supportive of these conclusions.

6. I have discussed this in more depth in *Power and Influence: Beyond Formal Authority* (Kotter [1985]). There are examples in that book of leadership from the supervisory level all the way up to the CEO level.

7. Unfortunately, a considerable amount of the research on leadership also focuses on these indices, and without systematically taking into account differences in context or setting, that produces an endless series of seemingly contradictory findings. See Bass (1981).

   There is also confusion because effective leadership can be difficult to measure precisely, especially the agenda-setting aspect. It can often take years to tell if a person who was successful in mobilizing a group of people actually led them in a sensible direction. This is one reason why historical and longitudinal studies of leadership are so important.

8. Fred Fiedler (1967) was one of the pioneering researchers to make this point and to try to develop a simple theory that encompassed this insight. Also see my (1982) discussion of this in *The General Managers*, Chapter 5, and Bass's (1981) discussion in *Stogdill's Handbook of Leadership*, Chapter 4.

9. See, for example, the work of Vroom and Yetton (1973), and Hershey and Blanchard (1977).

10. This discussion was launched in a provocative article by Professor Abraham Zaleznik (1977) of Harvard.

11. For more information on Geneen, see Allen (1980).

12. And some people think its "ethical performance" has been very poor at times, too.

13. See Kotter (1982), especially Chapter 4.

## Chapter 3 (*pp. 28–40*)

1. The essence of complexity is great interdependence among very diverse elements. I have spelled out some of the implications of complexity in organizations in greater detail in my last book. See Kotter (1985), especially Chapters 2–6.

2. These conclusions draw heavily on my study of effective general managers (see Kotter [1982], Chapter 3, especially Figure 3.1), and on additional work by Bentz (1985), Gabarro (1986), Isenberg (1984), Kaplan (1984, 1986), McCall and Lombardo (1983), Sayles (1979), and Boyatzis (1982).

3. See David McClelland's work, especially McClelland, (1975).

4. I have described the requirements for effective leadership in middle and lower level professional and managerial jobs in some depth in *Power and Influence*, Kotter (1985).

5. This was one of fourteen "principles of management" originally stressed by Henry Fayol. Almost all conventional management texts stress the point. See, for example, Scanlan (1973).

6. A lack of integrity eventually undermines network building activities. See Kaplan's (1984) discussion of this point.

7. That is not to say that no one develops leadership attributes other than some intellectual skills in school. People do; the young man who learns something about the interpersonal dynamics of leadership because he was captain of the football team is an obvious example. But those are exceptions instead of the systematic product of an educational institution.

8. A more elaborate discussion of these issues, based on an empirical study of a group of successful general managers, can be found in Chapter 3 of Kotter (1982). Also see McCall, Lombardo, and Morrison (forthcoming).

9. See Kotter (1982), Chapter 3.

10. The number of MBA graduates per year has gone up tenfold, while the amount of executive education offered by universities has grown even faster. Sources: The AACSB and Bricker Executive Education Service.

## Chapter 4 (*pp. 43–55*)

1. A fictitious name (and disguised industry details) for a well-known firm.

2. This and other information about the firm comes from interviews conducted in 1979 and 1981.

3. The reference is to ice hockey.

## Chapter 5 (*pp. 56–62*)

1. For further evidence and discussion of the dynamics shown in Exhibits 5–2 to 5–5, see Thompson, Kirkham, and Dixon (1985), pp. 21–23; Graves (1980); Kaplan, Kofodimos, and Drath (1986); Hamel and Prahalad (1986); and McCall, Lombardo, and Morrison (forthcoming).

## Chapter 6 (*pp. 63–75*)

1. Both the measurement and the access problems are overwhelmingly complicated.

2. Because more than half of the respondents worked in just seventeen firms, the data from those seventeen firms were compared to the rest of the questionnaire data to see if there were any significant differences. (If significant differences existed, that would suggest that the seventeen firms were somehow an unusual sample.) No such significant differences were found.

3. When administering early versions of the questionnaire, we found that people other than those who were subsequently polled often felt they did not have sufficient information to answer many of the questions.

4. Reported in the December 9, 1985, edition of *Fortune*, p. 207.

5. Reported in the January 1985 edition of *Fortune*.

6. Mostly "good."

7. For example, the Executive Resources Questionnaire data may distort reality in a number of ways. Although those polled were instructed to skip any questions they did not have sufficient information to answer validly, some people probably provided answers in areas in which they were not well informed. And equally well-informed people may well have provided different responses sometimes because of their different internal standards. This type of survey is also susceptible to the so-called halo effect.

8. As measured by the Fortune Reputation Study.

Chapter 7 (*pp. 79–94*)

1. The highest ranking any firm would receive based on the Executive Resources Questionnaire and the *Fortune* Reputation Study would be "very good."

2. For example, the range of mean responses (per firm) to Question 58 in the Executive Resources Questionnaire from more than six hundred executives in seventeen corporations was 34 to 70 percent.

3. There are obvious limits to this analysis because of the type of data involved and the way they were collected. Nevertheless, it provides some systemic basis for exploring important, but potentially elusive, questions.

4. The survey was first launched in 1983 and reported in January 1984. A second survey was reported in January 1985, a third in January 1986, and a fourth in 1987. The January 1985 survey was used here.

5. This assertion gets additional support from the questionnaire study. Two firms were in both the ER Questionnaire study (more than twenty executives in each filled out the survey) and the Best Practices Study. Those two firms received firm scores in the survey that were much above the overall mean for that survey.

6. There was one exception in which only three executives were interviewed.

7. For example, in the 1960s and early 1970s, when the vast majority of large commercial banks did not recruit at the Sloan School at MIT or Harvard Business School, Citicorp was on both campuses with great visibility. At Harvard, it recruited every year, even years when it had no compelling reason to spend extra money on high-potential recruiting. Its officers readily accepted speaking invitations, even interviews for the campus newspaper. It allowed many cases to be written about it, including some that most corporations would never have allowed because the cases exposed "problems" the bank was facing. But, as a result, Citicorp attracted during those years more Harvard MBAs than almost all other major commercial banks combined. Among the people it attracted at Harvard during those years was Tom Theobold, now the second in command at the bank. It also found John Reed (the current chairman) at MIT.

8. During the background interviews, executives in firms with reputations for poor leadership often said the main way they developed managers was by means of training.

9. See, for example, Chapter 3, especially Table 1, in Shaeffer (1984).

10. See Peters and Waterman (1982).

11. See McCall, Lombardo, and Morrison (forthcoming).


## Chapter 8 (*pp. 95–108*)

1. The conclusions drawn in this chapter are based mostly on information from interviews done in conjunction with the development of this book.

2. As measured by the *Fortune* Reputation Study.

3. There is almost universal agreement on this point among organizational sociologists and psychologists. See, for example, Schein's (1985) recent discussion of culture.

4. GE under Reg Jones staffed well over 90 percent of its executive positions with insiders. Today, under Jack Welch's leadership, that has dropped down somewhat, but the percentage is still high.

5. IBM has the same policy, yet spends even more money on management training. In the recent past, IBM has sent virtually all of its 42,000 managers to forty hours of general management training *each and every year*—training that focuses on "leadership." They have also sent managers off-site for another forty hours of more specialized or issue-oriented training each year.

6. GE policy has allowed managers to reject an entire slate. But one would do this only on a rare occasion without drawing unwanted attention.

7. Ed Schein (1985) has recently argued that the most important thing a CEO can do is to help maintain or change his corporate culture. This conclusion is not inconsistent with what we have found here.

8. See Siehl and Martin (1984).

9. From Werssowetz and Michael Beer (1982), p. 8.


## Chapter 9 (*pp. 109–121*)

1. All names are disguised.

2. I personally have encountered more than a dozen variations on this story and have had other people describe an additional dozen.

3. It is still too early to tell how successful these efforts will be, but initial signs look good.

4. A disguised name.

## Chapter 10 (*pp. 122-133*)

1. A detailed discussion of these issues can be found in Clawson et al. (1986).

2. For a good discussion of the forces involved, see Porter (1986).

3. Some are obviously much more internationalized than others (Citicorp, Coca Cola).

4. The Japanese, once again, were the first to exploit this possibility aggressively. They purchased thousands of licenses, mostly from American firms, even during the 1960s.

5. The best known case on record of turning around a senior management team is Chrysler. That appears to have required three years. As of this writing eight years after Iacocca was hired, the firm is still trying to build the kind of lower- and middle-level management it wants and needs.

# Bibliography

Allen, Steven A. "International Telephone and Telegraph Co. (A)," HBS Case Services, #9-472-007. 1980.

Bass, Bernard. *Stogdill's Handbook of Leadership*. New York: Free Press, 1981.

_____. *Leadership and Performance Beyond Expectations*. New York: Free Press, 1985.

Bennis, W., and Burt Nanus. *Leaders*. New York: Harper & Row, 1985.

Bentz, J. "View of the Top." Unpublished manuscript, 1985.

Bower, Joseph. *When Markets Quake*. Boston: Harvard Business School Press, 1985.

Boyatzis, Richard E. *The Competent Manager*. New York: John Wiley, 1982.

Burns, J. M. *Leadership*. New York: Harper & Row, 1978.

Carroll, G. R. "Dynamics of Publisher Succession in Newspaper Organizations," *Administrative Science Quarterly*, 29 (1984): 93–113.

Clawson, Jim, John Kotter, Charles McArthur, and Victor Faux. *Self-Assessment and Career Development*. 2d edition. Englewood Cliffs, N.J.: Prentice-Hall, 1986.

Fiedler, F. *A Theory of Leadership Effectiveness*. New York: McGraw-Hill, 1967.

Gabarro, J. J. *The Dynamics of Taking Charge*. Boston: Harvard Business School Press, 1987.

Gamson, W. A., and N. A. Scotch. "Scapegoating in Baseball," *American Journal of Sociology*, 70 (1964): 69–72.

Graves, J. Peter. "Management Behavior and Career Performance." In Brook Derr (ed.), *Work Family and Career*. New York: Praeger, 1980.

Grusky, O. "Managerial Succession and Organizational Effectiveness," *American Journal of Sociology*, 69 (1963): 21–31.

Hamel, Gary, and C. K. Prahalad. "Unexplored Routes to Competitive Revitalization." Working Paper Series #14, Center for Business Strategy, London Business School, July 1986.

Hershey, P., and K. H. Blanchard. *Management of Organizational Behavior*. 3d edition. Englewood Cliffs, N.J.: Prentice-Hall, 1977.

Iacocca, Lee, and William Novak. *Iacocca: An Autobiography*. New York: Bantam Books, 1984.

Isenberg, D. J. "How Senior Managers Think," *Harvard Business Review*, 62 (November–December 1984): 81–90.

Jennings, E. E. *An Anatomy of Leadership: Princes, Heroes, and Supermen*. New York: Harper & Brothers, 1960.

Kaplan, R. E. "Trade Routes: The Manager's Network of Relationships," *Organizational Dynamics*, Spring 1984, pp. 37–52.

_____. "The WARP and WOOF of the General Manager's Job," Technical Report #27. Greensboro, N.C.: Center for Creative Leadership, 1986.

Kaplan, R. E., Joan Kofodimos, and Wilfred Drath. "Development at the Top: A Review and a Prospect." In W. Pasmore and R. W. Woodman (eds.), *Research on Organizational Change and Development*. Greenwich, CT: JAI Press, 1986.

Kotter, John P. *The General Managers*. New York: Free Press, 1982.

_____. *Power and Influence: Beyond Final Authority* New York: Free Press, 1985.

Kotter, John P., and Paul Lawrence, *Mayors in Action*. New York: John Wiley, 1974.

Levinson, Harry, and Stuart Rosenthal. *CEO: Corporate Leadership in Action*. New York: Basic Books, 1984.

Lieberson, S., and J. F. O'Connor. "Leadership and Organizational Performance: A Study of Large Corporations," *American Sociological Review*, 37 (1972): 117–30.

McCall, M. W., Jr., and M. W. Lombardo. "What Makes a Top Executive," *Psychology Today*, February 1983.

McCall, M. W., Jr.; M. M. Lombardo; and Ann M. Morrison. *The Lessons of Experience*. Forthcoming.

McClelland, David. *Power: The Inner Experience*. New York: Irvington Publishers, 1975.

Peters, Tom, and Robert H. Waterman, Jr. *In Search of Excellence*. New York: Harper & Row, 1982.

Porter, Michael (ed.). *Competition in Global Industries*. Boston: Harvard Business School Press, 1986.

Prahalad, C. K. "Developing Strategic Capability: An Agenda for Top Management," *Human Resource Management*, 22 (1983): 237–54.

Salancik, G. R., and J. Pfeffer. "Constraints on Administrative Discretion: The Limited Influence of Mayors on City Budgets," *Urban Affairs Quarterly*, 12 (1977): 475–98.

Sayles, L. R. *Leadership: What Effective Managers Really Do . . . and How They Do It*. New York: McGraw-Hill, 1979.

Scanlan, Burt. *Principles of Management and Organizational Behavior*. New York: John Wiley, 1973.

Schein, E. H. *Organizational Culture and Leadership*. San Francisco: Jossey-Bass, 1985.

Scott, Bruce, and George Lodge. *U.S. Competitiveness in the World Economy*. Boston: Harvard Business School Press, 1985.

Shaeffer, Ruth Gilbert. *Developing Strategic Leadership*. Conference Board Report No. 847. 1984.

Siehl, C., and J. Martin. "The Role of Symbolic Management: How Can Managers Effectively Transmit Organizational Culture?" In J. G. Hunt, D. Hosking, C. A. Schriesheim, and R. Stewart, (eds.), *Leaders and Managers: International Perspectives on Managerial Behavior and Leadership*. New York: Pergamon Press, 1984.

Thompson, Paul, Kate Kirkham, and Joan Dixon. "Warning: The Fast Track May Be Hazardous To Your Health," *Organizational Dynamics*, Spring 1985.

Tichy, Noel M., and Mary Anne Devanna. *The Transformational Leader*. New York: John Wiley, 1986.

Vroom, Victor H., and Philip N. Yetton. *Leadership and Decision Making*. Pittsburgh: University of Pittsburgh Press, 1973.

Werssowetz, Richard O. von, and Michael A. Beer, "Human Resources at Hewlett-Packard," HBS Case Services, #482-125. 1982.

Zaleznik, A. "Managers and Leaders: Are They Different?" *Harvard Business Review*, 55, no. 5 (1977): 67–80.

# Index

SOUTHEASTERN COMMUNITY COLLEGE LIBRARY

3 3255 00062 9288

SOUTHEASTERN COMMUNITY
COLLEGE LIBRARY
WHITEVILLE, NC 28472

HD 57.7 .K67 1988

Kotter, John P.

The Leadership Factor

SOUTHEASTERN COMMUNITY
COLLEGE LIBRARY
WHITEVILLE, NC 28472